Contents

Series introduction	v
How to use this book	vi
Topic introduction	vii
1. Arguments about English	**1**
1.1 How we feel about language	2
1.2 Standard English	5
1.3 Non-Standard English	7
1.4 The origins of Standard English	8
1.5 The development of Standard English	10
1.6 Complaints about English	12
1.7 Changing English	14
2. Technology and language	**25**
2.1 Technology and language change	26
2.2 Technology and new words	31
2.3 Attitudes to texting	34
2.4 Attitudes to other forms of CMC	41
2.5 Emoji	42
3. Attitudes to language variation	**47**
3.1 Variation: what it is and what it ain't	48
3.2 Attitudes to regional variation	51
3.3 Attitudes to other varieties	67
4. Language discourses	**73**
4.1 Analysing language discourses	74
4.2 Describing language	75

4.3 A language toolkit	79
4.4 Further exploration and investigation	92
Ideas and answers	**94**
References	**99**
Glossary	**103**
Index	**106**
Acknowledgements	**107**

Cambridge Topics in English Language

Attitudes to Language

Dan Clayton
Series Editors: Dan Clayton and Marcello Giovanelli

CAMBRIDGE
UNIVERSITY PRESS

University Printing House, Cambridge CB2 8BS, United Kingdom

One Liberty Plaza, 20th Floor, New York, NY 10006, USA

477 Williamstown Road, Port Melbourne, VIC 3207, Australia

314–321, 3rd Floor, Plot 3, Splendor Forum, Jasola District Centre, New Delhi – 110025, India

79 Anson Road, #06-04/06, Singapore 079906

Cambridge University Press is part of the University of Cambridge.

It furthers the University's mission by disseminating knowledge in the pursuit of education, learning and research at the highest international levels of excellence.

www.cambridge.org
Information on this title: www.cambridge.org/9781108402149

© Cambridge University Press 2018

This publication is in copyright. Subject to statutory exception and to the provisions of relevant collective licensing agreements, no reproduction of any part may take place without the written permission of Cambridge University Press.

First published 2018

20 19 18 17 16 15 14 13 12 11 10 9 8 7 6 5 4

Printed in Great Britain by CPI Group (UK) Ltd, Croydon CR0 4YY

A catalogue record for this publication is available from the British Library

ISBN 978-1-108-40214-9 Paperback

Cambridge University Press has no responsibility for the persistence or accuracy of URLs for external or third-party internet websites referred to in this publication, and does not guarantee that any content on such websites is, or will remain, accurate or appropriate.

....

NOTICE TO TEACHERS IN THE UK

It is illegal to reproduce any part of this work in material form (including photocopying and electronic storage) except under the following circumstances:
(i) where you are abiding by a licence granted to your school or institution by the Copyright Licensing Agency;
(ii) where no such licence exists, or where you wish to exceed the terms of a licence, and you have gained the written permission of Cambridge University Press;
(iii) where you are allowed to reproduce without permission under the provisions of Chapter 3 of the Copyright, Designs and Patents Act 1988, which covers, for example, the reproduction of short passages within certain types of educational anthology and reproduction for the purposes of setting examination questions.

Series introduction

Cambridge Topics in English Language is a series of accessible introductory study guides to major scholarly topics in the fields of English language and linguistics. These books have been designed for use by students at advanced level and beyond and provide detailed overviews of each topic together with the latest research in the field so as to provide a clear introduction that is both practical and up to date.

In all of the books in this series, we have drawn on examples of spoken and written language. We hope these will encourage you to apply the theories, concepts and methods that you will learn in the books to analyse data and to think critically about a number of issues and debates relating to language in use. Many of the books also draw on data from the Cambridge Corpus. Throughout each book, you will find short activities to help develop reading and writing skills, longer extended activities and practice questions that will enable you to explore your learning in more detail and research findings that will provide inspiration for your own language investigations. Each of the chapters includes suggested wider reading, and a full glossary and reference section at the end of each book will support you to extend your learning and provide avenues for future reading and research.

We hope that each book will give you a good overview of its topic and, that taken as a whole, the series will map out some of the most interesting and diverse areas of language study, providing you with fresh thinking and new ideas as you embark on your studies.

Dan Clayton

Marcello Giovanelli

How to use this book

Throughout this book you will notice recurring features that are designed to help your learning. Here is a brief overview of what you'll find.

> **Coverage list**
> A short list of what you will learn in each chapter.

> **KEY TERM**
> Definitions of important terms to help your understanding of the topic.

> **ACTIVITY**
> A clearly defined task to help you apply what you've learnt.

> **RESEARCH QUESTION**
> A longer task to help you go deeper into the topic.

> **PRACTICE QUESTION**
> To give you some practice of questions you might encounter in the exam.

Ideas and answers
Further information, suggestions and answers to all activities and practice questions in the book.

Wider reading
Key texts to help extend your learning.

Topic introduction

What is 'good English'? You might think it involves spelling words correctly or speaking words that make perfect sense to others and carry a certain prestige or formality. Perhaps it involves avoiding language that might upset or offend another person or using a style and tone of voice that means others take you seriously.

From a very early age, we are given a clear sense that language is important not just to communication but to how we are judged and judge others. This comes through interaction with our parents and caregivers when we are very young, through teachers at school as we grow older but also through the attitudes we see and hear expressed about language in the media and wider society. We might be picked up on our language by others, criticised for the ways we use certain expressions, corrected online for typos or grammatical slips. Everyone has something to say about language.

Language provokes strong feelings because it is all around us all the time – it performs many functions and stands for so many things. It informs, persuades and entertains us but it also tells us a lot about the people who use it: where they are from, how they wish to appear to others and even some of their values and beliefs.

Attitudes towards different aspects of language are covered in this book. In Chapter 1, you will look at some background to debates about English and the roots of many of the contemporary arguments that rage. In Chapter 2, you will consider the role of technology in changing language and how these changes have been discussed. Chapter 3 focuses on language variation and diversity up to the present day, exploring attitudes to accents, dialects and the language used by different social groups. Finally, Chapter 4 offers ideas and frameworks for analysing how people use language to discuss language and text examples to explore linguistically.

Dan Clayton

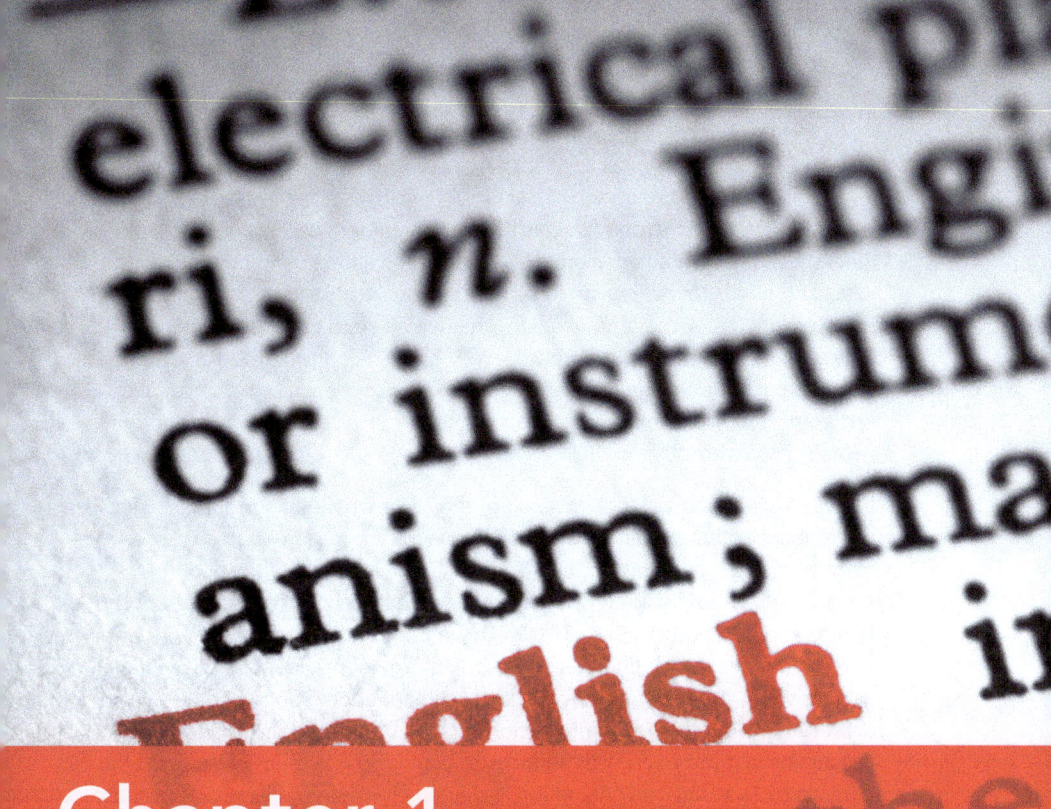

Chapter 1
Arguments about English

In this chapter you will:

- Consider some of the main debates about English
- Look at the origins of arguments about English
- Examine contemporary examples of arguments about English use

1 Attitudes to Language

1.1 How we feel about language

Language provokes strong feelings in so many people because it does so many different things. On a very simple level, language allows us to communicate ideas and needs that we have, to others. It allows us to express the desire to have a drink, eat something, explain what we'd like to do in the evening or how we feel about a particular book or TV show. Alongside this very important functional role, language also says a great deal about each of us: where we are from, how we want to project an image of ourselves, our values and our relationships with others.

In this chapter, you will look at some of the arguments that surround language use and the attitudes that are expressed towards language. As you will see, many of these arguments appear, on the surface at least, to be about topics such as new words, slang terms, the changes that technology makes to how we communicate and the ways in which we use accents and dialects, but once we dig a bit deeper we find that many of the arguments simply use language as a cover for other arguments. So, an argument about young people's use of abbreviations in online communication such as WhatsApp or Instagram might actually have more to do with attitudes to young people themselves – and the differences between one generation and another – than the language they use. As James Milroy and Lesley Milroy (1985: 45–46) put it:

> Language attitudes stand proxy for a much more comprehensive set of social and political attitudes, including stances strongly tinged with authoritarianism, but often presented as 'common sense'.

Later in this chapter you will look at how Standard English might be defined and how it emerged, but first have a look at some of the battlegrounds for language and the reasons for conflict.

ACTIVITY 1.1
Non-Standard English

Look at the list and consider each example of language use. Have you heard, read or used any of these expressions in any situation before? Score each one on a scale of 0–5 for how positively or negatively you feel towards each usage, with 0 as the most negative and 5 as the most positive.

- We done that yesterday
- The players gave everything they had; they done good
- And she was literally crying her eyes out

- Man's gotta earn ps innit
- And they come over to ours last week too
- #YOLO
- LOL, i no…
- You've got to listen to this track – it's sick

Whatever your feelings about these examples, there are some clear patterns to the language being used in them so that while the specific examples might change year to year, or decade to decade, the same kinds of complaints generally emerge about grammatical variation.

> **KEY TERM**
>
> **Grammatical variation:** how varieties of English use different grammatical structures to create meaning

1.1.1 Grammatical variation

Using 'done' for 'did' or 'come' for 'came' are often features of non-standard varieties of English, linked to regional dialects or sociolects. Likewise, the use of an adjective (*good*) where an adverb might be used in Standard English (*well*) might be linked to region or social class variation. A more recent grammatical development in some urban British varieties is the emergence of *man* being used like a pronoun instead of its more traditional noun role.

> **KEY TERMS**
>
> **Dialect:** language associated with a particular locality, region or geographical area
>
> **Sociolect:** language associated with a particular social group

1.1.2 Semantic variation

Complaints often arise out of words that change meaning or that are used to mean different things. This is known as semantic variation. 'Literally' being used to mean 'metaphorically' (as in the expression, 'When she left, my heart

Attitudes to Language

was literally broken in two' which doesn't 'literally' mean this at all – the consequences would be fatal – but is being used as a form of intensification or hyperbole) is not a recent development but has provoked much discussion in the last decade. Likewise, the process of flipping words, as in the case of 'sick' being used as a term of approval, is not a recent phenomenon (as anyone old enough to remember the release of Michael Jackson's *Bad* album could tell you). The use of cliché or dead metaphors such as 'gave everything' might also be an issue of semantics.

> **KEY TERMS**
>
> **Semantic variation:** how word meanings vary from place to place and group to group
>
> **Flipping:** a term used to describe a rapid semantic change in a word from one meaning to its opposite or near opposite

1.1.3 Orthographical variation

Orthographical variation, for example in acronyms (such as 'LOL' for 'Laugh(ing) Out Loud' or 'YOLO' for 'You Only Live Once') or other abbreviations (such as 'no' for 'know') provoke strong feelings among many people, but are frequently used in online contexts without any communicative problems. The changing role of punctuation symbols such as the octothorpe (or hashtag #) and ellipsis dots (…) could also come under this category.

> **KEY TERM**
>
> **Orthographical variation:** how the use of symbols, letters and spellings varies among language users

Other aspects of language provoke complaint too, such as phonological variation, but this is difficult to convey in the printed word on the page. Certain regional accents (often those associated with historically urban and economically deprived areas such as Birmingham and Liverpool in the UK, or Baltimore and south central Los Angeles in the USA) often cause strong negative reactions, being rated as less trustworthy and/or intelligent than apparently more prestigious accents, while certain characteristics of speech such as rising intonation or vocal fry lead to some negative judgements. Why should any of these examples provoke complaint? These judgements vary from place to place as well, because what is 'normal' for one group or place might be seen as novel or odd by others.

Arguments about English

KEY TERMS

Phonological variation: how the sounds of English vary among different speakers of English

Rising intonation: using a rising tone as an utterance ends. Generally used when asking a question, but now more prevalent in statements. Can also be referred to as High-Rising Terminals or Uptalk

Vocal fry: a way of speaking that constricts the vocal cords and creates a creaking, low frequency sound

RESEARCH QUESTION
Researching media representations of language

Choose a year in the last two decades and, using a range of media websites (e.g. *The Guardian*, *The Huffington Post*, *The Independent*, Slate.com, *Daily Telegraph*, Mail Online), identify the main stories that offer opinions about language. Can you categorise the main topics or areas that give rise to concerns about language use? For example, are some of them about accent prejudice, new words in the dictionary, or texting and literacy? What kinds of concerns are raised and how are these expressed?

You can develop this research task as the book goes on in order to identify possible data for analysis of language debates and for a potential language research investigation or project, so you can treat this as a step on the way to a more complete data set.

1.2 Standard English

All of the examples in Activity 1.1 vary from what might be seen as the norm for English language in ways that mark them out as non-standard: in other words, they are not examples of Standard English. But what exactly is Standard English and what is it for?

The linguist David Crystal explains that the role of a standard language is 'to enable the members of a community to understand each other' and that 'the leading national institutions, such as the British parliament, the US Congress, the BBC, and CNN, adopt it as their primary means of expression, in the interests of universal comprehensibility' (Crystal 2005: 6).

1 Attitudes to Language

Defining Standard English is perhaps less easy. According to sociolinguist Janet Holmes, a standard variety of a language 'is generally one that is written, and which has undergone some degree of regularisation or codification (for example, in a reference grammar and a dictionary); it is recognised as a prestigious variety or code by a community' (Holmes 2008: 76).

Standard English is not a static, unchanging form of language either. There have been significant changes over time to what might be viewed as Standard English – changes that are likely to continue into the future – and different standard forms exist around the world. So, for example, Standard American English and Standard Australian English exist as standard forms in their respective countries. Importantly too, very few people are brought up with Standard English as their home dialect and most of us will use non-standard varieties when we speak or we communicate online.

To even call Standard English a dialect is to open up part of its history to scrutiny. As you will see later in this chapter, Standard English first emerged from particular areas of England and from particular social groupings in England at the time, so it is linked to the history of the language and to the country's political and social history. As a result of being chosen as a prestigious form of English by a powerful group in society, Standard English carries with it (and can be used to exhibit) many connotations of power and authority. Some would even see Standard English as a superior form of English because it has power and authority, and the apparent ability to confer this power to others.

We are generally taught to use Standard English during our years in the education system and, whatever our social or geographical background, are encouraged to view it as the prestige form of our language: a standard to aspire to in our formal communication with others.

Standard English is generally regarded as possessing certain grammatical and lexical characteristics that make it suitable for its role as a shared language that all can understand. As such, it is seen to follow the widely accepted 'rules' of English. These 'rules' are not genuine linguistic rules, but more like conventions that are agreed upon, however. As language academic Jean Aitchison explained in her Reith Lectures for the BBC in 1996:

> All languages have their "rules" in the sense of recurring subconscious patterns. In English, we usually place the verb inside the sentence, and say: "The spider caught the fly". In Welsh, the verb comes first: "Caught the spider the fly" (Daliodd y pryf copyn y gleren), and in Turkish it comes last, "The spider the fly caught". Without these rules, communication would break down. But real "rules" need to be distinguished from artificially imposed ones.

1.3 Non-Standard English

While Standard English proves itself quite difficult to define, non-Standard English is a little simpler: anything that is not Standard English. This means that a range of grammatical variations would be seen as non-standard in most cases, such as:

- **Multiple negation:** using more than one negative marker in a clause, e.g. *we <u>didn't</u> see <u>nothing</u>* or *I'd <u>never</u> say <u>nothing</u> bad about him*

- **Subject–verb discord/lack of agreement:** using a verb form that does not match the standard person or number of the subject, e.g. *<u>we was</u> hoping* or *<u>she were</u> a great sister*

- **Marking/not marking tense:** using a form of a verb that is not generally seen to be a standard way of indicating the past tense, e.g. *he <u>come</u> up here yesterday* or *we <u>done</u> grammar at school today* (as my daughter told me after a day of grammar tests in school).

As a language student, you are discouraged from using terms such as 'incorrect' or 'bad English', so 'non-standard' is viewed as a less judgemental, more descriptive, term but it is clear that many people would see such usage as wrong. Some have even argued that the users of such non-standard expressions are ill-educated, ignorant or even immoral.

ACTIVITY 1.2
Ghetto grammar

Read Text 1A and consider the views about non-Standard English put forward. What objections is the writer raising about the uses of English that he dislikes and what views is he putting forward about the speakers of such language?

Text 1A

> Acceptance of "ghetto grammar" amounts to a betrayal of young people, trapping them in stereotypes. The young people I mentor are not stupid – yet their street slang makes them sound stupid and uneducated.

1 Attitudes to Language

> The better they speak, the more others – especially in positions of authority – will be inclined to take them seriously. Embracing street slang leads to disenfranchisement, marginalisation and ultimately the dole queue. Embracing "proper English" unlocks an intellectual feast.
>
> Extract from 'Ghetto grammar robs the young of a proper voice', Lindsay Johns (*Evening Standard*, 16 August 2011)

In this text, Johns makes a number of claims about the reactions people might have to what he calls 'ghetto grammar', including comments about employability, intelligence and education. Such views – and the language used to express them – are commonplace and will be explored in later chapters, but the idea that using non-Standard English limits and holds back its users is one that has been in circulation ever since there has been a Standard English to diverge from.

1.4 The origins of Standard English

Standard English did not appear by chance, despite many of its key elements gradually emerging over the history of the language. While attempts had been made in the Anglo-Saxon period to promote a standard in the form of the West Saxon dialect, this proved short-lived and for much of the time between the tenth and fifteenth centuries, other languages – Latin and then French – provided the prestigious forms to which educated people aspired and in which most written communication took place. In the case of Latin, this was due in part to its role in religious texts (some of the most widely read texts of the time) and in the case of French, this was due to the Norman invasion of 1066 and the influence of French-speaking rulers on the population of Britain.

By the fifteenth century, English had managed – against some considerable opposition – to achieve more prestige as a language in its own country: an idea that may appear odd to us now, given the subsequent spread and influence of English all over the world. According to Terttu Nevalainen and Ingrid Tieken-Boon Van Ostade (2006), King Henry V used English in his letters home while fighting in France during the Hundred Years War and at the same time Chancery English (the Chancery being what we might see now as a branch of the government's civil service) was becoming more widespread as the role of the written word and the subsequent need for agreed standards in writing began to grow.

The form of English used by Henry V is widely believed to have been the East Midlands dialect of English, so at some point a conscious decision would probably have been made to choose this. Figure 1.1 shows the areas of England that influenced Standard English at that time.

Arguments about English

Arguments usually given to explain this development are that this dialect was spoken by the largest number of people, that the east midland area was agriculturally rich, that it contained the seat of government and administration as well as the two universities of Oxford and Cambridge, that it contained good ports and that it was close to the chief archiepiscopal see, Canterbury. (Nevalainen and Tieken-Boon Van Ostade 2006: 275)

Figure 1.1: Map showing the 'triangle' of London, Oxford and Cambridge, the key areas in the south east and east Midlands that influenced Standard English

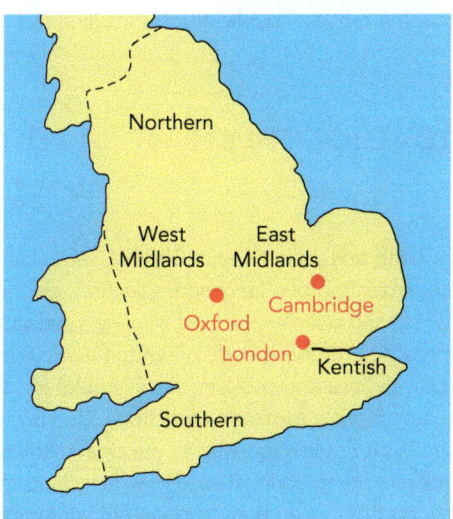

While these economic and political factors clearly had an influence on the selection of the East Midlands dialect as the developing standard form of English, other developments were probably responsible too. Professional writers and scribes – *scriveners* – were part of a growing middle class, who viewed the written word as a crucial means of conducting trade and government. As the written word grew in influence, a standard form, made up of many shared elements of English dialects around the UK, started to come together.

> For the basis of a standard language to have emerged so quickly, during the fifteenth century, its roots must have been present in a broad cross-section of society. There must have been a growing sense of shared usage, as individual scriveners (a term recorded from the end of the fourteenth century) with different backgrounds came into contact and began to influence each other. (Crystal 2005: 229)

At this point, it is important to point out that the emerging standard form was not entirely uniform. Standardisation is a process rather than a one-off event, and a process that continues to this day. It is clear for example that spelling

1 Attitudes to Language

has become more standard over time and this is something that had started to standardise by the sixteenth century (although not entirely, if stories about the six different ways Shakespeare spelled his name are to be believed) and continues to be discussed and debated to this day. Written texts from this time show a range of different spellings:

> In a single page one might read of *coronation* and *crownacion*, of a *rogue* and a *roage*, and of something that has *been*, *bin* or *beene*. (Hitchings 2011a: 69)

Moves were made in the eighteenth century to standardise grammar and word meanings through a range of publications, including dictionaries and grammar guides.

1.5 The development of Standard English

David Graddol, Dick Leith and Joan Swann (2006: 83–84) identify four key processes in the standardisation of a language: selection, elaboration, codification and implementation. Having selected the East Midlands dialect as the emerging standard, writers produced a growing body of written work in many different fields (religion, science, politics and cookery, for example) allowing the standard to be elaborated across different forms and functions. Codification came into play as time went on. With English growing in prestige, many attempts were made to draw up sets of rules to codify its use in written (and sometimes spoken) forms. Between the sixteenth and eighteenth centuries, dictionaries and grammars of English flourished and various pronouncements were made about the 'correct' way to use certain structures of English or (perhaps more often) the 'incorrect' and 'inelegant' usages to avoid. Among these, Bullokar (1586), Cawdrey (1604), Swift (1712), Johnson (1755), Lowth (1762) and Murray (1795) are perhaps the best known authorities of their time and more can be read about them in the suggestions for wider reading at the end of this chapter.

> It is difficult to assess how successful the eighteenth-century legislators were in achieving their aim of suppressing variation in language. They seem to have been successful in codifying a set of conventions appropriate for the written language – conventions which have not changed greatly since that time. The orthography, for example, has changed very little since Dr Johnson codified the spelling in his dictionary. Clearly, they were answering the need of a developing nation for reliable communication in writing, and in this they have been generally successful. (Milroy and Milroy 1985: 28–29)

In establishing a model for written English, spread through the now largely printed word (Caxton's printing press appearing in the UK in 1476), an ideology or way of thinking about English was taking root and it was written English that provided this model.

> **ACTIVITY 1.3**
> **Why have a standard?**
> Why is having a standard form of a language important? Think about the various benefits of having an agreed form of a language and the implications for individuals and institutions. What might be the problems faced without a standard form of a language? Alternatively, can you see any potential drawbacks to having a standard form?

Many of the arguments you will look at in this chapter and the rest of the book are focused on how English is used more widely than just formal, written communication. It is perhaps no surprise that once a standard has been set and conventions broadly agreed, other forms of language are often seen as substandard if they do not follow that standard, even if at times they are actually more widely used than the so-called standard form.

Much of this argument derives from different perspectives about language use, which can be broadly classified as prescriptive or descriptive. In the Cambridge Topics in English Language series, *Language Change* explores the historical development of these positions and approaches in more detail, but it is probably simplest to suggest that a prescriptive approach tells us what we should be doing with language (*prescribing* a way of using language), while a descriptive approach tells us how language is actually used (*describing* its features, functions, users and nature).

> **KEY TERMS**
> **Prescriptivism:** a way of viewing language as correct or incorrect, prescribing a 'correct' way to use language
>
> **Descriptivism:** a way of viewing language as being standard or non-standard, not making judgements about correctness

The eighteenth-century grammarians, whose books on the language shaped the perception of what Standard English should be, were largely prescriptive in their outlook. They often made reference to forms of grammar or vocabulary that people should avoid and offered examples of what they saw as 'proper' or 'elegant' language. It was an understandable position to adopt at the time, especially considering the relatively recently acquired status of English as the national language.

1 Attitudes to Language

Many of the grammarians saw the diversity of English – its accents, dialects, variable spellings, common turns of phrase – as being wild and out of control, and sought to 'cultivate' the language, much as a gardener might try to keep nature in check and make it attractive to others.

> **RESEARCH QUESTION**
> Researching the 'grammarians'
>
> Find out what you can about the ways in which each of the following people tried to exert an influence on the development and use of the English language. Which areas of language were they concerned about and how did they propose regulating them?
>
> - Jonathan Swift
> - Robert Lowth
> - Lindley Murray
> - Samuel Johnson
>
> To help you with this, you could use some of the following sources, which offer insights into the work of each of the writers, or check the wider reading section at the end of this chapter for further suggestions:
>
> - Baugh and Cable (2012) *A History of the English Language*
> - Crystal (1997) *The Cambridge Encyclopedia of the English Language*
> - Crystal (2005) *The Stories of English*
> - Hitchings (2011a) *The Language Wars: A History of Proper English*

1.6 Complaints about English

Even before this wave of concern about English, people had complained about the standard of the language. Jean Aitchison (1996: 4) refers to a '14th-century monk' who complained that 'the English practised strange "wlaffyng, chytering, harryng, and garryng grisbittyng" (strange stammering, chattering, snarling and grating tooth-gnashing)'. Robert Lane Greene (2011: 24), writing about William Caxton's frustration at finding so many different dialect words for the same thing (in this case, 'eggs') quotes the printer as saying, 'Certainly it is hard to please every man by cause of diversity and change of language'.

Arguments about English

What is it about the English language that makes so many people appear so concerned for its health and future? Perhaps it is not the language itself, but its users. In many ways, concerns about language decline are natural in that they are generational. In other words, each generation will see the language used by the next as different – and potentially deficient – compared to their own. Even young people can feel like this about those even younger than them. How do you feel, for example, about the language you hear spoken by those who are five to ten years younger than you? Do you ever feel that younger people's slang is embarrassing or childish?

A different perspective is to suggest that the language itself is resistant to regulation. As linguist Kate Burridge puts it, 'language is simply not amenable to being forced into standard moulds'. She explains:

> Speech communities are extremely complex and language has to cover a huge range of social behaviour. Yet, variability and mutability – qualities intrinsic to any linguistic system – do not sit happily within the classifications of a pure and consistent standard variety. The label 'standard' entails not only 'best practice' but also 'uniform practice' and this is only practical in the context of the written language, especially formal written language. (Burridge 2004: 11–12)

Spoken language is very different to written language: it varies much more from place to place and person to person, it does different jobs, is used in different situations and takes different forms. The range of different varieties of spoken language is huge: just look at the different dialects of the UK and varieties of World Englishes to get a sense of this. Websites such as those of the British Library can provide a useful starting point. Also, we have historically used speech when face to face with our conversational partners and in casual, spontaneous talk we often make it up as we go along, adopting grammatical structures that are quite different to those of written communication.

Alongside the spoken word itself, the context of communication is often more fluid, with the opportunity to refer to the immediate environment (for example, by pointing at things around us), respond quickly to questions or requests for clarification and shape meaning together using interaction.

The language of formal, written communication is not suited to many forms of spoken interaction, yet people are often judged on their spoken language using the standards of written language. And in some ways, it could be argued that spoken language has the potential to mean *more* than written language because spoken language is often a more multi-modal and social act where the literal meanings of the words and grammatical structures used are perhaps not as significant as the act of talking to someone, the body language of those involved and the implied meanings of the conversation taking place.

1 Attitudes to Language

1.7 Changing English

English has continued to develop throughout its history. New words are added all the time, new meanings emerge, ways of pronouncing words and sounds shift from person to person and place to place, and grammar looks quite different in some contexts to how it did in the past.

Increasingly, as you will see in Chapter 3, advances in technology now mean that some forms of computer-mediated communication (CMC) use many dimensions of the spoken mode in a form that is still read through the visual channel (so still a kind of writing). Do the rules of eighteenth-century Standard English still apply to the language of Facebook, Twitter and Snapchat?

KEY TERM

Computer-mediated communication (CMC): any form of communication that uses the medium of a keyboard or digital device, rather than being spoken or written

ACTIVITY 1.4
Spelling study

Investigate the ways in which words are spelled in texts from different times. First, choose a set of words to research and use the British Library website to check the spelling of these words from different periods of history. What variations do you notice? Are spellings more regular in printed texts in the twenty-first century?

Then take a range of messages from different people using social media platforms and apps such as WhatsApp, Snapchat, Facebook, Twitter and text messages. (Make sure you ask permission before you use the messages.) Study a sample of these and identify any examples of non-standard spelling, punctuation and grammar. What patterns do you notice? How standard is spelling now compared to previous centuries?

Figure 1.2 is a screenshot from the Cambridge Learner Corpus, which consists of answers to written tests from students all over the world (in this case, First Certificate in English (FCE) tests). What do you notice about the common spelling mistakes in these responses?

Arguments about English

Figure 1.2: Spelling mistakes in answers to FCE tests

areas, good food, and friendly <#DN><#S>	sorrounding	| *surrounding* </#S>| *surroundings* </#DN> - it
Radiant didn't <#FV> *played* | *play* </#FV> for 35 <#S>	minuts	| *minutes* </#S> in all, as the report explains
might have gone cut <#RT> *by* | *on* </#RT> our <#S>	bicyles	| *bicycles* </#S> . Unfortunately <#MP>
to <#UD> *the* | </#UD> school by <#S>	bicycle	| *bicycle* </#S> , <#RP> *A* | *a* </#RP> car collided
, <#RP> *A* | *a* </#RP> car collided with her <#S>	bicycle	| *bicycle* </#S> , and this accident <#DV> *gave*
<#DV> *gave damage to* | *damaged* </#DV> her <#S>	bicycle	| *bicycle* </#S> . She can no longer ride her
bicycle </#S> . She can no longer ride her <#S>	bicycle	| *bicycle* </#S> after that incident. Therefore
<#RN> *idea* | *plan* </#RN> and we didn't buy a <#S>	bicycle	| *bicycle* </#S> . Moreover, there is
more which I want you to know. In my <#S>	contry	| *country* </#S> it's impossible to ride <#MD>
impossible to ride <#MD> | *a* </#MD><#S>	bicycle	| *bicycle* </#S> or motorbike because of our
roads for riding <#MD> | *a* </#MD><#S>	bicycle	| *bicycle* </#S> . Anyway, <#RC> *so* | *because* </#RC>
of the <#R> *most* | *worst* </#R> problems of <#S>	ur	| *our* </#S> town. <#RY> *Especially* | *Particularly*
old buildings to save their historical <#S>	charakter	| *character* </#S> . In general we must combine
<#R> *According to* | *Having seen* </#R> your <#S>	advertisment	| *advertisement* </#S><#RT> *on* | *in* </#RT> the London
</#RP> at my old club in Stockholm. I <#S>	belive	| *believe* </#S> it's very important for everybody
to do some <#UN> *sport* | </#UN><#S>	exercis	| *exercise* </#S> to keep <#UA> *them* |
Because I'm <#MD> | *a* </#MD> very <#S>	buzy	| *busy* </#S> man, my <#R> *working time is almost*
</#R> and we've <#W> *got* <#FN><#UP><#S>	managment-meeting	| *management-meeting* </#S>| *management meeting*
Sincererly | *Sincerely* </#DY> The most <#S>	embarrasing	| *embarrassing* </#S> moment of my life was
the murdered woman wasn't Martine but <#S>	sorried	| *sorry* </#S> for the other woman who was murdered

Attitudes to changes in modern English follow many of the same patterns already observed in this chapter: changes are often seen as a form of degradation and decay, and much change is viewed as a kind of decline from a pinnacle of perfection at some distant point in history. As Aitchison (2012) argues, such a prescriptive mindset does not reflect the true nature of language change, but neither does a more scientific 'evolutionary' model of change proposing that some languages or characteristics of them are inherently 'better'. In fact, to talk about language – or varieties within a language – being better or worse than others is to miss the point.

> The quasi-religious conviction of gradual decline has never entirely died out. But from the mid nineteenth century onward, a second, opposing viewpoint came into existence alongside the earlier one. Darwin's doctrine of the survival of the fittest and ensuing belief in inevitable progress gradually grew in popularity [...] The former lead(s) to an illogical idealization of the past, and the latter to the confusion of progress and decay with expansion and decline. (Aitchison 2012: 236–237)

Robert Lane Greene (2011) has argued that such declinist views simply fail to acknowledge the reality of language around them:

> A hundred and forty years ago, one in five Americans was illiterate. Now less than one in a hundred is—and this fall began during a hundred years of "separate but equal" dismal schools for blacks in America. In Britain, illiteracy is rarer still. It may be true that formal grammar was taught more extensively in good schools in the past. But the notion that once upon a time, every schoolboy was an H.W. Fowler, every schoolgirl a perfectly punctuating Lynne Truss, but today no one can put two words together simply holds no water. Where is the former golden age of the written word? (Greene 2011: 47)

Attitudes to Language

> **KEY TERM**
>
> **Declinism:** a tendency noted by Robert Lane Greene for prescriptivists to view language as being in a state of constant decline from a once great peak

It is undeniable however that the speed of certain forms of language change has increased in recent years as a result of the internet and digital communication, so concerns about language change have tended to match this pace. Articles complaining about new words entering the dictionary and new meanings emerging for old words, along with pieces bemoaning the apparent disappearance of the full stop and apostrophe from young people's writing are all part of the linguistic landscape. As you will study in more detail in Chapter 4, many of these concerns are phrased in similar ways and draw on familiar discourses, but here you can look at some of the main trends.

1.7.1 Vocabulary change

New words appear in order to describe new things, but also to describe and label new concepts or beliefs. From its earliest days, English has added to its lexicon, often taking words from other languages, the process of borrowing what are then called loan words. This way of describing it led one commentator to ironically suggest, 'We don't just borrow words; on occasion, English has pursued other languages down alleyways to beat them unconscious and rifle their pockets for new vocabulary' (Nicoll 1990).

> **KEY TERMS**
>
> **Lexicon:** the vocabulary of a language
>
> **Borrowing:** the process of taking a word from another language and inserting it into the lexicon of another
>
> **Loan word:** a word that has been borrowed

Borrowing is well recognised now and, in many cases, English speakers are unaware that the words they treat as normal English vocabulary once came from abroad. Try looking up words such as 'alcohol', 'pyjamas', 'bungalow', 'assassin', 'skill' and 'tattoo' for evidence of their linguistic origins. However, lexical imports from Greek and Latin created some concern in the late fifteenth to early sixteenth centuries in what became known as the 'Inkhorn Controversy'. 'Inkhorn terms' – those imports that were judged to be pretentious or unnecessary, including words such as 'democracy' and 'impede' – were debated and 'purer' Anglo-Saxon derived alternatives proposed.

While the controversy was a clear example of a public debate about the nature of English language change, many of the words earmarked for rejection are still used today, and this is a common trend: attempts to regulate the language and control its use are generally doomed to failure. However, the same argument – that of protecting the 'purity' of English from outside forces – is still advanced in the present day, often with what are seen to be American English words identified for rejection.

For example, in his article 'Say no to the get-go!' the journalist Matthew Engel (2010) complains about the term 'from the get-go' which he describes as 'an ugly Americanism, meaning "from the start" or "from the off". It adds nothing to Britain's language but it's here now, like the grey squirrel, destined to drive out native species and ravage the linguistic ecosystem'.

In a different article on the same theme, Engel (2011) addresses a range of other words he deems to be American imports, citing 'lengthy', 'reliable', 'talented', 'influential' and 'tremendous' as US English. However, only one of these ('lengthy') is recognised as such by the linguist Mark Liberman (2011) and Engel's attack is described by Liberman as a form of 'language peeving': a venting of irrational prejudice with little basis in fact.

Other complaints about new words follow a similar pattern. When words enter one of the recognised dictionaries, there is a flurry of media attention, often focusing on the novelty of these new terms and the perception that they will be short-lived and faddish. Some commentators argue that only 'proper words' should be recorded in a dictionary (single words rather than phrases or compound nouns, and words rather than emojis, as Oxford Dictionaries did in 2015 with the 'face with tears of joy' emoji 😂 becoming their word of the year) and that they should be serious, substantial words that are set to last. Quite how anyone can tell which words will last is not entirely clear!

KEY TERM

Emoji: a term to describe visual icons (representations of facial expressions, actions and objects) used in social media messaging

Christopher Howse (2010) argued that:

> … it is very easy to concentrate on neologisms that reflect the wilder shores of modern life. It's harder to spot defining markers of the way we live now. At the moment the temptation is to identify too many trends from new media – web-surfing, blogging, twittering and unfriending.

Attitudes to Language

But if those terms are in fact the ones that most accurately represent the language used at a given time, why shouldn't they appear in a dictionary?

> ### ACTIVITY 1.5
> Words of the year
>
> Using the websites of the following dictionaries, put together a list of the 'words of the year' for the last five to ten years. What patterns do you notice in terms of the way they are formed and the processes that have created them? Are they blends, compounds, initialisms, acronyms or clippings, for example?
>
> Then look for media articles from around the same time as these words entered the dictionaries. What opinions have been offered about these new words and their suitability for inclusion?
>
> Suggested sources:
>
> - Oxford Dictionaries
> - Macmillan Dictionaries
> - Collins Dictionaries
> - Merriam-Webster Dictionaries
> - Macquarie Dictionaries

It is not just neologisms and new words in the dictionary that provoke anger in some commentators. The appearance of particular words in speech, such as 'like' used as a filler (as in 'I was like so upset and she was just like so uncaring') has led some journalists to describe the speech of those who use such features as inarticulate and vacuous. The actor Emma Thompson even went so far as to say in an interview in 2010 that young people should not use such features in their language: 'Just don't do it. Because it makes you sound stupid and you're not stupid.'

> ### KEY TERMS
> **Neologism:** a completely new word
>
> **Filler:** a word or sound used to fill a gap in spoken language (e.g. *um, err, uh, like*)

However, appearances can be deceptive, and while the use of 'like' as a filler has probably increased – influenced by US usage, perhaps – the same word has

Arguments about English

also been used in other ways. 'Like' can also function as a quotative (as in 'I was like "What did you say?" and she was like "Nothing!"'), so while it might be used more by particular groups of people, it is also being used in different ways.

Semantic changes in existing words can also cause concern. While you are probably familiar with how established slang terms such as 'sick', 'wicked' and 'bad' are all flipped or ameliorated forms of their original meanings, many other words have gone through a gradual process of semantic change in which their meanings have gone through narrowing to become more precise, broadening to encompass more meanings, or pejoration to pick up more negative connotations.

Words such as 'awful' and 'awesome' have shifted over time. While 'awful' is believed to have once meant 'worthy of respect or fear' (with its meaning linked to its component 'awe') it is now widely perceived as meaning 'very bad' (as in 'Did you see that accident outside college? It was awful.'). 'Awesome' has moved in a different direction, from being used to describe something that provoked fear, terror or respect to a more modern meaning that expresses approval (e.g. 'I loved that film; it was awesome.').

While these are relatively gradual changes to language, prescriptivists often argue that changes in meaning can lead to a lack of intelligibility between the different generations, with younger speakers seeing a word as having a meaning that is completely at odds with how an older generation might view it.

KEY TERMS

Quotative: a language device used to convey what was said, thought or done in an interaction (e.g. she *said*... or she *was like*...)

Amelioration: the process of a word's meaning changing and picking up more positive connotations over time

Narrowing: the process of a word's meanings becoming more specialised over time

Broadening: the process of a word's meanings becoming more generalised over time

Pejoration: the process of a word's meaning changing and picking up more negative connotations over time

Intelligibility: the ability to be understood and comprehended

'Literally' is another example of a word that has been used in different ways. On one level, 'literally' can mean 'to the letter', where it is the opposite of 'figuratively' or 'metaphorically', but it can also mean its exact opposite (see Figure 1.3).

1 Attitudes to Language

Figure 1.3: 'Literally' or 'figuratively'? Cartoon from xkcd webcomic

In an article responding to the decision by some dictionaries to include the 'figurative' definition, Samantha Rollins (2013) explains it as follows:

> As anyone who paid attention in grade school knows, "literally" means "in a literal or strict sense, as opposed to a non-literal or exaggerated sense," and is the opposite of "figuratively," which means "in a metaphorical sense." But recently, it's become in vogue to use "literally" for emphasis in precisely the non-literal sense, as in, "We were literally killing ourselves laughing." It's the type of informal use that drives any self-respecting language lover nuts.

Again, there is more to this debate than meets the eye. 'Literally' has been used figuratively for hundreds of years and caused very little confusion. The lexicographer Michael Rundell (2011) points out that when examining corpus entries for the word, the meanings of 'literally' were generally very clear: 'Our corpus includes almost 30,000 examples of *literally*, and I've looked at a sample of 1000. The great majority reflect one of the unproblematic senses of *literally*.'

Elsewhere, the linguist John McWhorter compares 'literally' to other similar words with similarly expressive functions – 'really', 'very' and 'truly' – which have all undergone semantic change, shifting away from their original meanings. He also makes the point that many other words mean one thing and their opposite; there is even a name for these words – contronyms.

> **KEY TERM**
>
> **Contronym:** a word that can mean one thing and its exact opposite at the same time

You *seed* a watermelon to get the seeds out, but when you seed the soil, you're putting the seeds in. You can *bolt* from a room (running fast) in which the chairs are bolted to the floor (stuck fast). (McWhorter 2016: 26)

We understand the meanings of the words from their contexts, so rarely get genuinely confused.

> Asked to seed a watermelon, no one carefully removes the seeds from one watermelon and then inserts them into another. (McWhorter 2016: 26)

ACTIVITY 1.6
Semantic change

Are there any other words whose meanings have changed over time? Have any of these caused complaints? Look at the examples and see if any of these follow the same patterns that have been discussed.

- terrible
- heavy
- cute
- silly

1.7.2 Phonological change

Changes to the sounds of English have taken place over many hundreds of years, and in the Cambridge Topics in English Language series, *Language Change* offers more details on developments such as the Great Vowel Shift, while in this book, Chapter 3 will consider attitudes to different accents and dialects of the UK and beyond. More recent changes have led to some consternation on the part of language prescriptivists and those averse to innovation. As with so many other arguments about language, these are often more to do with the users of language than the feature itself.

We will consider one example in this section: high-rising terminals (HRT) but you might also want to look at Activity 1.7 at the end of the chapter, which asks you to examine media representation of vocal fry. Traditionally in English, the intonation of questions rises at the end of the utterance, but not the intonation of statements. Think of how you might say the following sentences aloud:

- Would you like some crisps?
- Was that your dad?
- Wasn't that amazing?

1 Attitudes to Language

> **KEY TERM**
>
> **High-rising terminals (HRT)/uptalk:** a way of speaking in which the intonation pattern moves up towards the end of a declarative utterance

When this intonation is used with statements, it becomes what has been referred to as uptalk. Try saying the following sentences as if you are asking a question with them:

- You like crisps.
- That was your dad.
- That was amazing.

Uptalk is generally viewed as a recent phenomenon and has been identified in a number of media articles over the last 20–30 years. Originally associated with 'Valley Girl' talk (speech associated with the San Fernando Valley in California, USA and popularised in the song 'Valley Girl' by Frank Zappa) and then with Australian accents (from which it has also gained the title Australian Question Intonation), its supposedly increased use among young people – and particularly young women – has attracted much comment.

Stefanie Marsh of *The Times* (2006) described it as 'this irritating verbal tic' while others have described English as being 'infected' with this style. And a cursory scan of YouTube videos about uptalk even suggest that it could make you physically sick.

One of the key complaints about uptalk for many commentators has been its association with uncertainty. If you make a statement sound like you are asking a question – the complaint often goes – you will sound uncertain about what you are saying. Many articles have been written advising women (and it is generally women who are the targets of these articles) on how to avoid using uptalk so as to not be judged as uncertain or unassertive.

A piece by Naomi Wolf (2015) asserted that 'the most empowered generation of women ever – today's twentysomethings in North America and Britain – is being hobbled in some important ways by something as basic as a new fashion in how they use their voices'. She argued that uptalk can 'undermine these women's authority in newly distinctive ways'.

Responding to this article, linguist Deborah Cameron (2015b) pointed out that it is not just young women who use uptalk, but that it is also used by older women and many men. While young women often lead linguistic innovation and are first to use a new speech feature, 'if everyone does uptalk, just to different degrees, then it doesn't make sense to interpret it as an expression of young women's lack of confidence and their reluctance to project authority. If that was what uptalk expressed, men wouldn't have followed women's lead by adopting it'.

It is no coincidence that women – and especially young women – have been singled out for attention with uptalk, because as Cameron points out in the same blog post, 'negative attitudes to the language of subordinate groups are just manifestations of a more general prejudice against the groups themselves. People may claim that their judgments are purely about the speech, but really they're judgments of the speakers'. As she goes on to say elsewhere:

> This endless policing of women's language—their voices, their intonation patterns, the words they use, their syntax—is uncomfortably similar to the way our culture polices women's bodily appearance. Just as the media and the beauty industry continually invent new reasons for women to be self-conscious about their bodies, so magazine articles and radio programmes like the ones I've mentioned encourage a similar self-consciousness about our speech. (Cameron 2015a)

Perhaps what is actually happening with uptalk is that the intonation pattern no longer means what it meant before. As words change meaning over time, so do sounds. In this case, uptalk is perhaps signalling a desire to cooperate in interaction, to check that someone else is following, or even to assert control over a conversation by making sure others are listening.

John McWhorter (2016: 36) explains it in the following way:

> … the meaning of an intonation can drift, via implication, just as the meaning of a word can. This includes questions. It's interesting how often what we couch formally as questions are meant as statements. If we ask someone who is piling their omelette with pepper "How much pepper do you *need*?" we are not waiting for them to specify how much. We are stating something, and something quite specific: that the person is overdoing it – here, using too much pepper.

And therefore uptalk is performing a role different to the role it performs when phrasing a question:

> If the uptalker is actually questioning anything, it is not the validity of her statement but whether the person listening understands or shares the same basis of knowledge and evaluations. (McWhorter 2016: 36)

Attitudes to Language

ACTIVITY 1.7
Examining vocal fry in the press

Investigate the media coverage of vocal fry and gather different texts about it. What do you notice about the ways in which it is represented and the advice offered to its users? This data will be useful when you reach Chapter 4 where you will study language discourses in more detail.

Wider reading

You can find out more about the topics in this chapter by reading the following:

Aitchison, J. (2012) *Language Change: Progress or Decay?* (Fourth edition). Cambridge: Cambridge University Press.

Crystal, D. (2005) *The Stories of English*. London: Penguin.

Milroy, J. and Milroy, L. (1985) *Authority in Language: Investigating Standard English*. London: Routledge.

Nevalainen, T. and Tieken-Boon Van Ostade, I. (2006) 'Standardisation'. In R. Hogg and D. Denison (eds) *A History of the English Language* Cambridge: Cambridge University Press, p. 275.

Chapter 2
Technology and language

In this chapter you will:

- Look at how technology has influenced changes in the English language
- Consider arguments about the impact of technology
- Explore and evaluate contemporary debates about technology and language

2 Attitudes to Language

2.1 Technology and language change

Technology has had a huge influence on how the English language has changed over time. However we choose to define technology – as tools for communicating or as digital devices – it has influenced not only the language we use but how we use it. On a very simple level, technology has allowed us to move beyond face-to-face communication into forms that allow us to speak almost instantly to someone on the other side of the world, to 'write' on a screen and send those words to thousands of people instantaneously, and to move beyond the two dimensions of a sheet of paper into a world of interactive hyperlinks, online comments and pictures of Shiba Inu dogs captioned in strangely phrased English. Doge and LOL cat memes use deliberately odd English to create a voice for the animal in the picture and to be playful with language. What makes the language appear strange? (See Figure 2.1 for an example.)

Figure 2.1: Example of a LOL cat meme

Technology is one of the main influences on the ways in which language develops in the twenty-first century, bridging gaps between people but sometimes putting up walls between others. It can offer us new ways to use language while amplifying old problems and is at once optimistically democratic in its uses as well as being dangerously totalitarian. At the start of the twenty-first century, journalists were celebrating the potential of the internet to offer us unlimited access to news and views, giving a voice to the marginalised and voiceless, yet now we are deluged with 'fake news' and vile racist and misogynistic abuse.

Technology has also opened up fault lines between those who believe it can improve literacy and disseminate knowledge and those who see it as a force that dumbs down language and lowers attention spans.

Technology and language

One perspective that we will return to later is offered by Tom Chatfield:

> ... many of the official intentions behind Standard English are already unofficially defunct. For the first time in history, we live in a culture not only of mass literacy (itself a relatively recent revolution), but of mass participation in written discourse. Online, reading and writing – which not so long ago were among the most costly and elite of human activities – are almost infinitely available at little or no cost. For better and for worse, we are no longer simply speakers of our own tongue: we are all becoming both authors and audiences. (Chatfield 2013: 3)

In this chapter, you will look at the ways in which technologies have influenced (and continue to influence) language, and the debates and arguments over the nature of those changes. As with the other chapters in this book, you will look at a range of different perspectives and will need to evaluate what you make of these ideas.

2.1.1 Writing technologies

All 'writing technologies', as linguist Dennis Baron refers to them, have caused some disquiet as they have developed.

> The World Wide Web wasn't the first innovation in communication to draw some initial scepticism. Writing itself was the target of one early critic. Plato warned that writing would weaken memory, but he was more concerned that written words – mere shadows of speech – couldn't adequately represent meaning. His objections paled as more and more people began to structure their lives around handwritten documents. (Baron 2009: x)

As Baron goes on to outline, the printing press was 'faulted for disrupting the natural, almost spiritual connection between the writer and the page' (2009: x), the typewriter was viewed as being too impersonal, too noisy and a bad influence on handwriting skills, while more recent technologies such as computers have been derided for 'speeding writing up to the point of recklessness, complicating it, trivializing it' and leading to too many people communicating about nothing.

Even the humble pencil was once viewed as a dangerous writing technology. Many of the arguments used by those on the prescriptive side of the debate have cropped up again and again for other technologies. Baron explains:

> Once people finally accepted the usefulness and authenticity of handwritten texts, or of words carved in stone, they balked at the new technology of printing, which threatened to both democratize reading and to depersonalize it. A few hundred years later, the typewriter upset our literary practices once again. It was bad enough that the clacking typewriter joined the equally noisy adding machine in the increasing mechanization that was permeating and, in the eyes of many, dehumanizing the modern

Attitudes to Language

office of the early twentieth century. Typewriters also threatened to render handwriting obsolete. (Baron 2009: 14)

The mechanisation of writing technologies brought with it concerns about humans losing their jobs and humanity somehow being lost amid the machinery. Many of these concerns are echoed in contemporary articles about robots taking the place of humans in all walks of modern life, whether it's car assembly lines or paralegals at law firms. Language aside, technology on its own has the potential to cause concern and this is amplified when it is shown to affect language and perhaps shape our identities. Concerns have also been raised about people's (often young people's) ability to use older writing technologies, such as the pen. Some commentators have suggested that children are starting school unable to master the grip on a pen which children ten or twenty years ago would have done as second nature. Many of these worries echo the ones you will look at later in the section on texting.

2.1.2 Speaking technologies

Technology hasn't just affected how we write but also how we speak. The telephone (invented in the late nineteenth century) allowed people to communicate by speech over long distances (hence its etymology: *tele* = far and *phone* = sound). Early telephones – in fact almost all telephones up to perhaps the turn of the twenty-first century – bore no resemblance to the mobile devices almost 5 billion people now use around the world.

Most telephones were situated in offices, homes and telephone boxes, affecting how people in many developed countries worked, and telephones are widely credited as one of the great technological advancements of the last 150 years. Language use with telephones developed its own rituals and expectations. Are these still relevant to personal calls made and received on mobile phones?

- The person receiving the call would identify themselves or the phone number that had been called (e.g. 'Hello, Winterslow 446688, Terry Clayton speaking'.)

- The person making the call would identify themselves (e.g. 'Hello, it's Phil from the Haxby Bakehouse calling').

- The sign-off or farewell would often involve set phrases such as 'thank you', 'speak to you again soon' or 'all the best'.

The sociologist Emanuel Schegloff identified four distinct sequences in dyadic (two-way) telephone calls:

- **summons – answer:** for example, a phone ring and some kind of response is offered in answer

Technology and language

- **identification – recognition:** the participants in the call identify each other
- **greetings:** more interactional or social greetings are used
- **initial inquiries ('how are you?'):** opening questions and social interaction open up the topic for discussion. (Schegloff 1986)

Technology has affected much more than the vocabulary and grammar of spoken language, but also the discourse structure of turn-taking and even the social behaviour of many people. The ritualised exchanges of such calls became the norm for telephone users brought up with the 'landline' but all of that has changed with the advent of mobile telephony, caller display and personalised ringtones for individual contacts. And here is one of the reasons why some argue that technology is a problem: change frightens people. If you are brought up to view one form of behaviour as 'right' and then see that changing among younger generations, you might well feel that what they are doing is 'wrong'. And language is just another form of behaviour that is subject to these concerns.

ACTIVITY 2.1
Telephone use

Study all the different ways in which you, and those around you, use phones to speak to others.

- How many calls do you make (if any)?
- How long are these calls?
- What are the functions of these calls?
- How do these calls match Schegloff's outline?
- Are calls ever made on speakerphone or using FaceTime (or an equivalent app)?
- Does this vary depending on age and gender?
- Are there any types of phone use that you find annoying?

Consider as well, other forms of speaking technology such as radio and television. Not only have these media brought us new forms of language and allowed us to communicate to new and ever bigger audiences, but they have also shaped the ways in which we respond to the world, what we talk about and how we experience particular types of talk: the celebrity interview, the post-match chat and the straight-to-camera newsreader's delivery, for example. None of these would be as familiar to us if TV and radio had not been invented.

2 Attitudes to Language

2.1.3 'Texting' technologies

One of the most interesting developments in technology has been the advent of what many call computer-mediated communication (CMC). Susan Herring (1996) refers to this as a form of 'communication that takes place between human beings via the instrumentality of computers' (Herring 1996: 1). In essence, the computer (be it a PC, a laptop, a tablet or mobile device) sits in the middle, between the text producer(s) and the text receiver(s).

CMC blurs the lines between writing and speech and offers a new form of communication that allows language to take a visual form (read through the visual channel, as traditional writing would be) but offering many characteristics of the spoken mode (conversation-like turn-taking through near-instant exchange of messages, often ephemeral and largely social in function). CMC has often been referred to as 'texting' even when it is not associated with traditional SMS-style texts through a phone, and this broader term often encompasses forms such as online messaging, tweeting and messaging through apps such as Snapchat and WhatsApp.

While speech and writing have never been fixed binary opposites (think for example of messages written on a sticky note and put on the fridge door, quickly scribbled shopping lists and the complex rhetorical structures of politicians' speeches), CMC has made the continuum between them more interesting. Linguist Naomi Baron describes CMC as resembling:

> speech in that it was largely unedited; it contained many first- and second-person pronouns; it commonly used present tense and contractions; it was generally informal ... At the same time, CMC looked like writing in that the medium was durable, and participants commonly used a wide range of vocabulary choices and complex syntax. (Baron 2008: 48)

Texting technologies have affected social behaviours including language. Many 'moral panics' – periods of raised media concern over the supposed ill-effects of a new phenomenon – have sprung up over texting. The issue of texting while driving had been on the front pages of many UK newspapers before legislation was passed to make it unlawful and texting while walking has led to concerns in the USA. Teachers regularly complain about students becoming distracted by their mobile devices in class and writers often spend too much time on Twitter when they should be finishing chapters of already-late books. Many concerns have been raised about the influence of texting on language skills and you will return to these later in the chapter.

Technology and language

> **ACTIVITY 2.2**
> **CMC use**
>
> Log your own use of CMC in a given day. How much time do you spend messaging, checking Twitter, using Instagram or on similar social media apps? Do you send emails as part of your normal working/studying day? Do you notice any distinct language styles that differ from platform to platform or device to device?
>
> If you keep track of your CMC messages and exchanges, you can build up a corpus of material to analyse in more detail as this chapter goes on or to use as part of a longer language investigation.

2.2 Technology and new words

One of the ways in which technology has made an impact on English is through its role in the creation of new words and repurposing of older words. As you have already seen in Chapter 1, attitudes to new forms of language vary enormously. On the one hand, new words are seen by many as being vital to describe and label new products and concepts, but on the other hand some object to new words, seeing them as faddish or throwaway and insignificant.

Many of the terms used to describe new technologies and what we do with them have given rise to debate and you will look at a few key examples in this section.

2.2.1 Lexical and semantic change

It is rare to see new words appear out of thin air and when they do they are generally termed neologisms. More often, new words are formed through various processes of combination: blending and compounding. For example, 'Facebook' is a compound of two existing words and gives each word a new slant. Is it your genuine 'face' that is presented through Facebook or a carefully curated version of it? Likewise, how is an online page really a 'book'? One of the most productive ways for technology to shape language is for it to invest old words with new meanings.

2 Attitudes to Language

> **KEY TERMS**
>
> **Blending:** the process of word creation by combining two elements of other words (e.g. 'bromance' = _bro_ther + _romance_; 'brunch' = _br_eakfast + _lunch_)
>
> **Compounding:** the process of word creation by combining two existing words either as a new single word, hyphenated word or noun phrase (e.g. 'laptop' = _lap_ + _top_; 'user-friendly' = _user_ + _friendly_)

'Twitter' is similar. Once used as a common noun to describe the song of birds, the social media platform harks back to this meaning with its blue bird logo and allows millions of users to tweet their own 'songs'… or frustrated responses to international politics and football results.

Figure 2.2: Example of tweets

Other words have undergone similar processes of semantic change:

- 'Virus': originally used as a medical term to describe a body causing infection, the word is now used to describe programs that can interfere with the normal running of a computer.

- 'Zombie': used to describe a kind of undead spirit but is now also used to describe a computer that has been infected with a virus and is under the control of an outside force.

Think about the following words and how they have been used in new ways to describe new technologies or technological practices:

hack	follower
patch	desktop
forum	troll
menu	stream
mouse	save

While all these words exist in their older forms, their new technological meanings have taken on a life of their own. These double meanings are not always accepted. As with much semantic change, some prescriptivists argue that new meanings create confusion and should be avoided. But the nature of language is that it will generally change to fill gaps that we need. Allan Metcalf notes:

> It seems a basic principle of language that if an expression is widely used, that must be because it is widely useful. People wouldn't use a word if they didn't find it useful. (Metcalf 2016)

This fits with what has been described as the functional theory of language change: that language changes to suit the needs of its users. This does not necessarily mean that language is changing to become more efficient or less complex. However, language is a tool of communication and humans have many and varied needs: we use language in a transactional function to convey ideas and emotions, but we also use it in an interpersonal function to express solidarity, social distance and identity. It might follow then that language changes to suit the many needs of its users in many different directions at once.

Guy Deutscher (2006) refers to three overarching patterns in language change:

- **Economy:** that language changes to save its users time and energy (e.g. abbreviations in texting, ellipsis on Twitter).

- **Expressiveness:** finding new ways to express or emphasise meaning when old ways lose power or effectiveness (e.g. needing to find new ways to say 'good' or 'great': *awesome, terrific, amazeballs*).

Attitudes to Language

- **Analogy:** that language changes in ways that match how other changes have taken place; that language changes because of cumulative changes made for similar reasons.

These forces pull in different directions. So, for example, while some changes brought about by technology might lead us to abbreviate and shorten aspects of words and syntax, other changes add new words and new meanings to our vocabularies. We are at once eroding language and building it anew.

2.2.2 Grammatical change

Functional shift or conversion can also take place to give older words new meanings and functions. One clear example of this is the use of the verb 'like' as a noun when referring to Facebook interactions. For example, a user might receive a number of 'likes' for a post, reflecting whether or not it met with approval from others. Another word, which seems to have undergone both a semantic and grammatical shift, is 'friend'.

> **KEY TERM**
>
> **Conversion:** the process of changing the grammatical function of a word (e.g. turning a noun into a verb or vice versa)

Tom Chatfield explains:

> The fact that a social network with around a billion registered accounts chose 'to friend' as its principal verb of interconnection has not so much shifted the older sense of the word as created an entirely new one – drawing attention in the process to both the social network's aspirations, and the gulf between its rhetoric and actuality. The word friend itself comes almost directly from the Old English verb *freond*, itself derived from the verb *freogan*, meaning to love or bestow favour upon. The idea of 'friending' as well as 'befriending' has been used as a verb for over half a millennium – but it wasn't until the public advent of Facebook in 2005 that its contemporary sense arrived. (Chatfield 2013: 201–202)

2.3 Attitudes to texting

Since the arrival of Short Message Service (SMS) or 'texting' in the late 1990s, the impact of this particular form of CMC has been discussed at length. Originally limited to 160 characters and expensive to use, texts often made use of the kinds of grammatical ellipsis seen in telegrams some 40–50 years previously ('Will arrive 4pm. Bring crisps') and what many saw as new forms of abbreviation ('C U L8er', 'thx m8' and 'wot u up 2').

These abbreviations were among the most contentious forms of language that texting gave rise to. The kinds of abbreviation often fall into particular categories:

- **Shortenings and clippings:** application – *app*, brother – *bro*, family – *fam*
- **Initialisms and acronyms:** *BRB* – Be Right Back, *IMO* – In My Opinion, *GF/BF* – girlfriend/boyfriend, *LOL* – Laugh(ing) Out Loud
- **Deviant spelling:** night – *nite*, light – *lite*, come – *cum*, over – *ova*
- **Letter and number homophones:** You – *u*, I see – *I C*, later – *l8er*, hater – *h8er*, too much – *2 much*

Much media attention was focused on these abbreviations, with a widespread belief that texting had 'invented' such a practice. Articles in UK newspapers in the early 2000s and in the USA a decade later often claimed that texting was rife with abbreviations and sloppy English. Writing in 2002, John Sutherland, Professor of English Literature at University College London, argued that texting 'masks dyslexia, poor spelling and mental laziness. Texting is penmanship for illiterates'; and journalist John Humphrys (2007) went much further when he described texters as 'vandals who are doing to our language what Genghis Khan did to his neighbours eight hundred years ago. They are destroying it: pillaging our punctuation; savaging our sentences; raping our vocabulary'.

But, as Crystal points out, texting did not invent these abbreviations.

> People have been initialising common phrases for ages. "IOU" is known from 1618. There is no difference, apart from the medium of communication, between a modern kid's "lol" ("laughing out loud") and an earlier generation's "SWALK" ("sealed with a loving kiss"). Texts omit letters too ... But this isn't new either. Eric Partridge published his *Dictionary of Abbreviations* in 1942. It contained dozens of SMS-looking examples, such as "agn" ("again"), "mth" ("month") and "gd" ("good"), 50 years before texting was born. (Crystal 2008: 9–10)

While the need for concision was apparent and the desire to abbreviate understandable, texters were not generally creating new abbreviations but making use of old ones and showing a degree of creativity in adapting these to a new medium. Of course, many abbreviations have been invented as well (and not just as part of texting but in online gaming and instant messaging, for example) but the foregrounding of abbreviations as one of the main features of texting is perhaps misguided. Studies of text messages have usually shown a low proportion of abbreviations actually used when compared to words spelt in their more standard forms.

Various studies, including Thurlow and Brown (2003), Lyddy *et al.* (2014), Ling and Baron (2007) and Wood et al. (2011) (all referred to in Kaplan (2016))

2 Attitudes to Language

have found that the percentage of abbreviations in text messages collected from people of various ages, from primary school to university student, ranges from as low as 3.2 per cent among American college students to 40 per cent among 8–12-year-olds in UK schools (but varying depending on age within that group). This could be because of changes in the technology itself (as you will see later), but could also be down to the users' needs and styles changing, or no actual problem in the first place.

Perhaps it is not the use of abbreviations that is the issue for those who complain about texting, but the supposed influence of texting on more formal kinds of writing. Many of the complaints about texting focus on how it leads to breaches of formality in communication between students and teachers, or workers and their employers.

An article by Krupnick in the *Seattle Times*, 'Texting slang invading academic work', likened such lapses in formality to wearing inappropriate clothing:

> Faculty members increasingly have expressed irritation about reading acronyms and abbreviations they often do not understand, said Sally Murphy, a Cal State East Bay professor and director of the university's general-education program. One e-mail to a professor started with, "Yo, teach," she said.
>
> "It has a real effect on the tone of professionalism," said Murphy, who also has seen younger instructors use the shorthand. "We tell them very specifically how this is going to affect them in life. It's kind of like wearing their jeans below their butt. They're going to lose all credibility." (Krupnick 2010)

It could be argued that texting has an influence on perceptions of appropriate formality in different forms of communication but there is no clear evidence to suggest that it negatively impacts upon literacy. In fact, research into texting has generally suggested that it either has some benefits or no effect at all. Wood et al. (2011) discovered in their study that students who texted more had slightly higher scores on tests that measured phonological awareness and had no negative effects on other aspects of literacy. Plester et al. (2009) found that the earlier a child got their first mobile phone, the higher their literacy scores. This does not necessarily equate to a causal effect – i.e. that texting definitely improves literacy – but it does to some extent undermine claims that texting has to be bad for literacy.

As David Crystal says:

> Some people dislike texting. Some are bemused by it. But it is merely the latest manifestation of the human ability to be linguistically creative and to adapt language to suit the demands of diverse settings. There is no disaster pending. We will not see a new generation of adults growing up unable to

Technology and language

write proper English. The language as a whole will not decline. In texting what we are seeing, in a small way, is language in evolution. (Crystal 2008)

Much of the debate about texting and literacy has moved on because texting itself has moved on. Texting is now linked to many other forms of messaging through mobile devices and the old predictive text programs that made it much simpler and quicker to abbreviate words have now been replaced.

Figure 2.3: Older phones made use of very basic predictive text while new phones are much more adaptive and intuitive

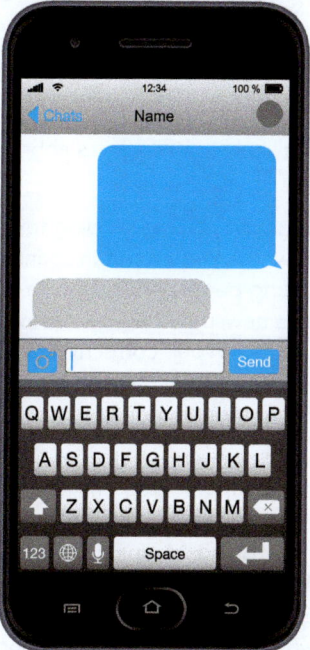

New applications can predict not just the word you are going to type next, but which word you would normally use after the last one that appeared. Apps like SwiftKey have been developed with the input of linguists and draw upon the language data of the user to predict a range of words that might appear next. By using a mini-corpus of language data for each user, the predicted text should be more personalised. But does this potentially run the risk of limiting users' vocabularies? If we are faced with predicted words that have been generated by a computer algorithm, will we just be satisfied with what is put in front of us, rather than think about a wider range of vocabulary that we might use? Will this shrink our vocabulary and make all communication a little more generic?

2 Attitudes to Language

> **PRACTICE QUESTION**
>
> **The impact of texting on literacy skills**
>
> Texts 2A and 2B put forward contrasting views about the impact of texting on people's literacy skills.
>
> Analyse how language is used to present views about technology and language.
>
> Evaluate the ideas in the sample texts and put forward your own case, based on your own study of English Language.

Text 2A

Michael Deacon believes that literature is likely to become as abbreviated as teenagers' attention.

Baroness Greenfield, the neuroscientist, is worried that sending text messages may cause young people to have shorter attention spans. If she's right, of course, none of those young people will be aware of this, because she expressed her views in a newspaper article of several hundred words, some of them long, all of them spelt correctly, and none of them using digits as substitutes for whole syllables. All terribly old-fashioned and out-of-d8. So they won't have read it.

In all probability, then, she's preaching only to the converted. None the less, I'm right behind her. Admittedly, I'm not in the least qualified to comment on whether text messaging can cause mental disorders, or whether predictive text – the ability of your phone to guess what you're going to say – will stunt your powers of self-expression, and make you less thoughtful and more error-prone. But I do know one thing. Reading text speak, or txt spk, makes my eyes water as if hit by a jet of lemon juice. And even if using text speak doesn't reduce your attention span, it suggests that you've already got a pretty damn short one.

What is the excuse for it? I know that keeping messages below a certain character count can make them cheaper, but anyone who has ever received a text from a teenage relative will know that, if brevity was their aim, they wouldn't insist on ending every sentence with a row of at least six exclamation marks.

Being the neurotic, prematurely aged pedant that I am, I always type out every word in full when I'm texting, as if I were going to submit the thing to a publisher rather than merely use it to let my girlfriend know I've caught the 18.46 from Victoria station. Unlike the teenagers relying on their predictive text (and substituting "book" for "cool" or "Smirnoff" for "poisoned", because the keys are the same), I even reread my texts to check for spelling and grammar errors.

Technology and language

Now, this may well make me a certifiable lunatic – indeed, Baroness Greenfield is welcome to use me as a subject for her next study of neurological disorders. But I still think what I do is better than inflicting such assaults on the English language as "ROFL" (Rolling On Floor Laughing) or "BBFN" (Bye Bye For Now) or "DMFYLOCIAIM" (Delete Me From Your List Of Contacts, I'm An Illiterate Moron).

And it's not as if all these jaunty acronyms are universally understood. A lot of people over the age of 30 seem to think that "LOL" stands for Lots Of Love, rather than Laughing Out Loud. Which creates all kinds of potential for inadvertent offence. ("Don't B upset, babe – UR new hairdo looks gr8. LOL.")

Mobile phone companies are only too delighted to indulge their customers' laziness. My own phone goes one better than predictive text and offers a selection of text message templates, so that I don't even have to bother typing out "I'm in a meeting" or "See you at…". There's even a template that says "Happy birthday". I wonder how little you'd have to think of a friend not just to send a text instead of a card, but to refuse to go to the effort of typing it.

Still, language is in a constant state of evolution. Perhaps text speak will seem perfectly normal in 50 years' time. Perhaps there'll be a 21st-century edition of Shakespeare's collected works featuring "2B/not 2B", and the *Oxford English Dictionary* will define "2thless" and "1derment". Perhaps misery memoirs will be written not in prose, but as a series of increasingly downcast emoticons.

But let's look on the bright side. If everyone in the world keeps texting, we'll all become as mentally stunted as each other, and so nobody will even notice that there's been a narrowing of the human attention span. Or, as it will surely become known, a10shn spn.

'Texting is making English a foreign language', Michael Deacon
(*The Telegraph*, 12 August 2009)

Text 2B

People have always spoken differently from how they write, and texting is actually talking with your fingers.

Texting has long been bemoaned as the downfall of the written word, "penmanship for illiterates," as one critic called it. To which the proper response is LOL. Texting properly isn't writing at all — it's actually more akin to spoken language. And it's a "spoken" language that is getting richer and more complex by the year.

First, some historical perspective. Writing was only invented 5,500 years ago, whereas language probably traces back at least 80,000 years.

2 Attitudes to Language

Thus talking came first; writing is just an artifice that came along later. As such, the first writing was based on the way people talk, with short sentences — think of the Old Testament. However, while talk is largely subconscious and rapid, writing is deliberate and slow. Over time, writers took advantage of this and started crafting tapeworm sentences such as this one, from The Decline and Fall of the Roman Empire: "The whole engagement lasted above 12 hours, till the gradual retreat of the Persians was changed into a disorderly flight, of which the shameful example was given by the principal leaders and the Surenas himself."

No one talks like that casually — or should. But it is natural to desire to do so for special occasions, and that's what oratory is, like the grand-old kinds of speeches that William Jennings Bryan delivered. In the old days, we didn't much write like talking because there was no mechanism to reproduce the speed of conversation. But texting and instant messaging do — and a revolution has begun. It involves the brute mechanics of writing, but in its economy, spontaneity and even vulgarity, texting is actually a new kind of talking. There is a virtual cult of concision and little interest in capitalization or punctuation. The argument that texting is "poor writing" is analogous, then, to one that the Rolling Stones is "bad music" because it doesn't use violas. Texting is developing its own kind of grammar and conventions.

Texting is developing its own kind of grammar. Take LOL. It doesn't actually mean "laughing out loud" in a literal sense anymore. LOL has evolved into something much subtler and sophisticated and is used even when nothing is remotely amusing. Jocelyn texts "Where have you been?" and Annabelle texts back "LOL at the library studying for two hours." LOL signals basic empathy between texters, easing tension and creating a sense of equality. Instead of having a literal meaning, it does something — conveying an attitude — just like the -ed ending conveys past tense rather than "meaning" anything. LOL, of all things, is grammar.

Of course no one thinks about that consciously. But then most of communication operates below the radar. Over time, the meaning of a word or an expression drifts — meat used to mean any kind of food, silly used to mean, believe it or not, blessed.

Civilization, then, is fine — people banging away on their smartphones are fluently using a code separate from the one they use in actual writing, and there is no evidence that texting is ruining composition skills. Worldwide people speak differently from the way they write, and texting — quick, casual and only intended to be read once — is actually a way of talking with your fingers.

All indications are that America's youth are doing it quite well. Texting, far from being a scourge, is a work in progress.

'Is Texting Killing the English Language?' John McWhorter (*Time*, 25 August 2013)

2.4 Attitudes to other forms of CMC

Many of the same arguments about texting are applicable to other forms of CMC. Indeed, 'texting' as a term is often loosely used to refer to many of these. Twitter had (at the end of 2016) 319 million active monthly users but has an influence way beyond those users, as many tweets are picked up in mainstream news publications, or tweets become news because of their controversial and/or provocative content or because of who has tweeted.

Twitter makes use of 140-character messages, so the need to be concise is paramount. However, users are not charged per tweet, as text messages generally were at the start of that technology. Twitter is also a potentially more interactive medium than texting because it allows online conversations to develop between multiple users. You do not need to 'follow' another user to be able to tweet them and while this has allowed more open discussion with users it has also led to unprecedented levels of 'trolling', where anonymous users (often described as 'eggs' because of the default Twitter egg icon used) can bombard others with abuse. This can range from the passive-aggressive process of 'sub-tweeting' or 'indirecting', which involves discussing or criticising someone without 'tagging' them in a tweet, to 'quoting' a tweet rather than replying to it (which allows some form of commentary on that tweet without it becoming part of a conversation between two users), through to direct confrontation by replying to another user.

Several high-profile cases in the UK have led to legal action being taken against the perpetrators of trolling and, in some cases, Twitter users have been jailed for their online actions. Some linguists and researchers have explored the role of online anonymity in shaping linguistic behaviour on platforms like Twitter and their findings are interesting to consider when thinking about the influence of technology on language use (and abuse). Has social media coarsened the standard of debate and led to instant, often angry, responses dashed off on a device without a thought for the recipient's feelings or the wider ramifications of the message that has been sent?

Claire Hardaker (2013) categorises a number of behaviours (that could be applied to a variety of CMC platforms such as online forums, Twitter and other social media) that might be identified by their recipients as 'troll-like', including deliberate digression from an agreed topic, aggression, antipathy and hypocrisy. These are not purely linguistic behaviours but are manifested through the medium of CMC so come under the remit of what is being explored here.

Is CMC, and Twitter in particular, degrading language? It might be part of a wider trend towards more confrontational and aggressive behaviour to strangers online, but that is perhaps more a social phenomenon than a linguistic one. When in 2011, the actor Ralph Fiennes complained that language 'is being eroded' by Twitter, his views were widely reported. But when linguistic studies have been carried out

2 Attitudes to Language

(Liberman 2011, for example, in response to Fiennes' claim) tweets have not produced any evidence of language degradation – quite the opposite in fact:

> A person tweeting has no option but concision, and in a backward way the character limit actually explains the slightly longer word length we see. Given finite room to work, longer words mean fewer spaces between them, which means less waste. Although the thoughts expressed on Twitter may be foreshortened, there's no evidence here that they're diminished. (Rudder 2014)

In Chapter 4, you will look in more detail at some of the discourses around language change, but this discussion of social media 'eroding' language is certainly a good one to come back to and consider.

2.5 Emoji

One of the main ways in which CMC has changed language is in its ability to make written language (or at least, typed/swiped language) closer to speech. As discussed earlier, online communication is close to some forms of spoken mode communication in its use of almost-synchronous turn-taking and frequently social and phatic interaction.

In fact, the words we use to describe online communication often come from the domain of speech. We have *conversations* online, we *chat* and we hit *reply*. But one thing that most online communication still doesn't offer is the tone of voice we can pick up from a genuinely spoken conversation. Tone is something that helps construct meaning, just as much as the words or the syntactical structures that we use and in CMC this is often missing. Emails, texts and tweets often miss their intended target or provoke unexpected reactions because a certain tone – sympathy, irony, exasperation – is missing in the words used. It is this area – generally referred to as part of pragmatics – that CMC often lacks.

> **KEY TERMS**
>
> **Phatic interaction:** the type of exchange which is redundant in terms of meaning but socially significant; it includes 'friendly noises' like 'Morning', 'Nice day' and 'How's things?'
>
> **Pragmatics:** the study of language as it is used in a social context

Linguist Caroline Tagg notes:

> ... internet users do not typically have access to the paralinguistic features (tone of voice in which something is said, for example), or to the facial expressions, gestures and body language of their interlocutors. The

Technology and language

implications of what is often thought of as 'impoverished' or deficient interaction are that people cannot express themselves as effectively as in spoken interactions; they are more likely to experience misunderstandings and they are more likely to feel less inhibited when it comes to confronting their unseen interlocutors. (Tagg 2015: 85)

For a while, emoticons offered a basic indication of tone. Simple punctuation marks could be used to signal:

- a smiling face :-)
- a sad face :-(
- a winking face ;-)

Punctuation can also be used in a non-standard way (!!!, ?!), caps lock used to sound louder (SEE YOU IN COURT!) and punctuation used to 'act out' certain words (*steps away from keyboard and weeps*). More recently, gifs (small, animated graphic files) memes (images, often accompanied with ironic or culturally-specific phrases such as "But the emails..." or "One does not simply walk into Mordor") and familar images have been used to signify reactions to others' online posts, with the 'facepalm' becoming a particular favourite to signal exasperation, incredulity or complete embarrassment at what someone else has just posted.

Figure 2.4: Jean-Luc Picard, the 'father' of the genre, shows the classic facepalm

Perhaps then, these visual images are a way of bridging the gap between CMC and true speech, providing tone and even a 'face' to online communicators.

Emoji (or *emojis*, depending on your preference) are another development in CMC and offer users the chance to add various facial expressions and small images. In their earliest incarnation, these were more developed, graphic

Attitudes to Language

versions of emoticons, but have now become a more diverse set of images. In 2015, the social network app Instagram reported that over half of its messages contained emoji (up from 10 per cent five years previously). Writing in *The Independent*, Adam Lusher commented:

> Pessimists may conclude that technology merely allows us to regress to a form of pictorial language which has more in common with ancient hieroglyphics than the alphabetic writing system pioneered by the Phoenicians in about 1,200BC. (Lusher 2015)

However, Instagram's Thomas Dimson, who led the research, appeared to have few such reservations. 'It is a rare privilege to observe the rise of a new language,' he said. 'On Instagram, emojis are becoming a valid and near-universal method of expression in all languages.'

Figure 2.5: The 'Face with tears of joy' emoji was Oxford Dictionaries' Word of the Year for 2015.

Are emoji a new language, as some have said? Probably not. Emoji can definitely assist communication but can they function as a separate language in their own right? Linguists Tyler Schnoebelen (2016) and Gretchen McCulloch (2016) have both argued in various interviews and articles (see Wider Reading) that while emoji can be sequenced, to be a true language emoji would need to be organised syntactically in a way similar to other human languages (which they aren't) and would be able to communicate sophisticated and abstract ideas (which they can't in their current form). But equally, are emoji damaging language and reducing it to a series of caveman-like hieroglyphics? This is unlikely and reproduces one of the 'declinism discourses' you will look at in more detail in Chapter 4.

RESEARCH QUESTION

Researching emoji

Text 2C is taken from an interview with linguist Vyvyan Evans for *Huck* magazine about his work on emoji. Read the text and consider the different ideas put forward. How would you go about conducting an investigation into the ways in which emoji are used? Come up with a methodology for exploring emoji use and see if you can think of how to gather your data, analyse it and evaluate your main findings.

Technology and language

Text 2C

However, many have been critical of emojis, dismissing them as facile or adolescent and fearing for the future of communication because of them. Although most of us can quite happily construct a sentence without having to resort to smiling-cat faces and aubergines, commentators such as Jonathan Jones foresee us abandoning the literary genius of Shakespeare for these "brainless little icons".

But as Vyvyan points out, this purist view of language has existed for as long as language itself and he believes that these prescriptivist preconceptions are doomed to fail.

"There's a misconception that language is something that doesn't change," he says. "But we don't speak the same English as Chaucer and new word coinages only get off the ground when people use them. In this regard, language is the great leveller – it's a living breathing organism that's constantly evolving."

"The problem is people are responding in a prejudiced way because [emojis] are cartoon-like. It's a gut response that lacks foundation."

What must be remembered when looking at emojis is that they aren't a language, but a facet of communication; they nuance language, rather than replace it. But Vyvyan believes that given the staggering increase in use of emojis over only a few short years, their evolution could see them become a language all of their own.

"It is possible for emojis to become a functioning language," he says. "You can look at blissymbols as an example of how language can be visually based; it's a symbol-based language that allows people with severe speech and motor difficulties to actively communicate with purely representational symbols, it's been particularly useful for many people with cerebral palsy."

However, before you go ahead and burn your dictionary, Vyvyan feels that in their current incarnation, emojis will not become a language.

"Emojis as we know them today have only been available since 2012, so this is still very recent," he explains. "Yet in such a short space of time emoji has become the world's global form of communication. In Silicon Valley they're already experimenting with animated emojis, so without trying to predict the future, it seems we could be seeing the foundations of a new language."

Extract from 'No, emojis aren't making our generation stupid',
Paden Vaughan (*Huck*, 16 January 2017)

2 Attitudes to Language

Wider reading

You can find out more about the topics in this chapter by reading the following:

Baron, D. (2009) *A Better Pencil: Readers, Writers and the Digital Revolution*. Oxford: Oxford University Press.

Chatfield, T. (2013) *Netymology*. London: Quercus.

Crystal, D. (2009) *Txtng: The Gr8 Db8*. Oxford: Oxford University Press.

Kaplan, A. (2016) 'Texting makes you illiterate'. In A. Kaplan, *Women Talk More Than Men… And Other Myths About Language Explained*. Cambridge: Cambridge University Press.

Tagg, C. (2015) *Exploring Digital Communication*. London: Routledge.

Gretchen McCulloch writes about emoji use in this Toast article from 2016: http://the-toast.net/2016/06/29/a-linguist-explains-emoji-and-what-language-death-actually-looks-like/

John McWhorter's TED lecture on texting provides a very useful overview: www.ted.com/talks/john_mcwhorter_txtng_is_killing_language_jk.html

Tyler Schnoebelen discusses emoji use in this 2016 interview on NPR: www.npr.org/2016/02/28/468483894/emojis-are-becoming-a-bigger-part-of-conversation

Chapter 3
Attitudes to language variation

In this chapter you will:

- Consider how regional and social variations in English are viewed
- Think about attitudes to non-Standard English
- Explore debates about these issues

3 Attitudes to Language

3.1 Variation: what it is and what it ain't

Language varies from person to person and place to place in many ways. Each of us has our own individual language style, known as an idiolect, and most regions of the UK and English-speaking countries around the world have their own recognisable dialect or variety of English. Language can vary on a number of levels:

- **Lexical and semantic variation:** words and meanings might be different in some parts of the country and the same words might actually have different meanings in one place compared to another (e.g. UK English 'trousers' and US English 'pants' refer to the same item of clothing).

- **Phonological variation:** sounds vary from place to place. Different regional accents exist around the UK, USA and other English-speaking countries, and speakers of languages other than English often pronounce sounds differently compared to many native speakers.

- **Grammatical variation:** some syntactical structures (such as word order for questions or negatives) vary across social and geographical boundaries, while morphology can also vary, with some varieties making use of markers for plurals while others don't.

- **Pragmatic variation:** beyond abstract differences in language, when people actually communicate face to face, they often draw on their own experiences of language rituals and interactions to create and understand meanings and these can vary as well. Attitudes to politeness in language – how, or whether, we use apologies or certain greetings or farewells – might be examples of this.

> **KEY TERM**
>
> **Idiolect:** variation in language use associated with an individual's personalised 'speech style'

For more detailed discussion about some of these variations, the Cambridge book *Language Diversity* (Clayton and Drummond, 2018) is recommended.

Attitudes to language variation

ACTIVITY 3.1
Discussing data

Look at the following examples of language data and consider how they might vary from the language you would use in a similar situation.

- We was just sat there, waiting.
- Your girl's got bare skills on Fifa, innit?
- How much did you get? I got nowt.
- She run fast fast.
- I ain't seen nobody come down here today. They come down yesterday but not today.
- Do you want butter on your cob, me duck?
- Nobody else thought he were funny, but I thought he were a right laff.
- This boy was like 'Where are you from?' and I was like 'Bow' and this is him 'Bow? These ain't your endz then' and this is me 'I'm visiting my cousin innit'.

Some of these examples illustrate the range of differences that exist between one group of people and another and from one geographical location to another, but equally, many other factors come into play here. While factors such as age and gender, along with regional and social background can influence our language, we all have choices about our language use. All of us 'perform' language in one way or another, depending on what we want to convey. In the same way that we can change our clothing to suit different occasions, we can change our speech to signal different social meanings and to perform different aspects of our identity. That might mean foregrounding more non-standard features to project a streetwise identity when with members of our peer groups or shifting into a more overtly prestigious form of Standard English when talking to authority figures who can exert a degree of influence or control on our lives.

Some linguistic variation is rooted in historical differences between the areas of the UK where different groups settled (see Figure 3.1). For example, in the north east of England, many place names are influenced by the language of the Vikings (Old Norse) who invaded and settled in those areas. Other linguistic variation is due to migration and immigration. One good example of this is the dialect of Liverpool in the north-west of England, where the linguistic influence of the Irish has had an impact on the local language. More recently, immigration from the Caribbean has influenced some of the language of young people from inner-city London and several other urban areas such as Bristol, Birmingham and Leeds.

3 Attitudes to Language

Figure 3.1: Sources of some of the influences on the English language

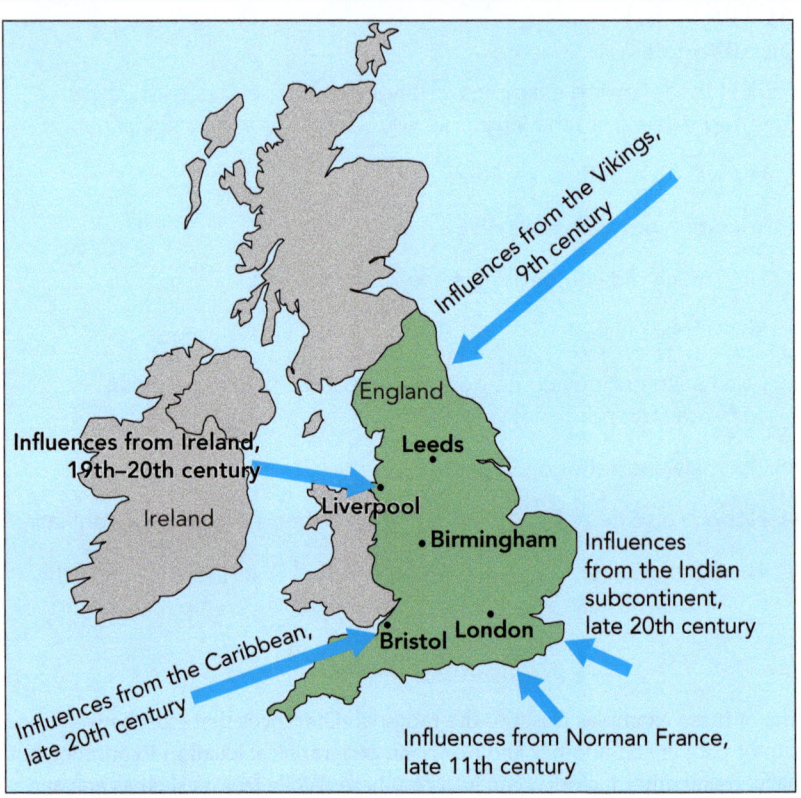

However, while such forms of variation are part of the history of English and contribute in many ways to the English we speak now, all over the world, there are strong feelings among many people – often amplified by influential media outlets – about the 'right' and 'wrong' ways to use language.

As you saw in Chapter 1, the gradual development and diffusion of a standard form of English led to one form of the language being granted more prestige and status than other forms, and it is perhaps this difference that underpins many of the attitudes that exist towards non-standard varieties. If they are not Standard English, they must be sub-standard, goes the argument. Linguists of course would disagree with this.

> Yes, there is a recognised standard variety of English, but this variety is simply another dialect, no better or worse than any other dialect of English. Its 'standardness' comes from status rather than quality, and this status was itself acquired indirectly through accidents of history. The truth is, as in all languages, the prestige variety is the variety associated with whoever happens to have the power in any given society. (Clayton and Drummond 2018:13)

Attitudes to language variation

Another reason why attitudes to language variation are so deep-seated is that they are not really about language at all but about the users of the language. Again we saw in Chapter 1 that attitudes towards language are often a 'proxy' for other – social and political – attitudes. As Henry Hitchings, author of *The Language Wars* puts it in an interview with 'emagazine' about debates around English language usage:

> These debates quickly become heated because they involve people's attitudes to – among other things – class, race, money and politics. (Hitchings 2011b: 26–27)

So, when some people complain about a feature of language – be it a 'like' in a teenager's speech, a 'like' used as a noun in social media communication, or 'likes' as a non-standard verb agreement in 'I likes it' – the complaint might be more about the social background of the language user than the language 'misuse' itself. It might also reflect the complainant's own social prejudices more than any linguistic issue.

3.2 Attitudes to regional variation

Negative attitudes to different regional dialects (including accent under the umbrella term 'dialect' here) are widespread and have been for centuries. In some ways this might just be a natural (if unfortunate) human tendency to identify differences in others and find something to ridicule in them, or perhaps it is connected to a sense of protecting one's own local and regional identity against those perceived to be outsiders. Even Chaucer and Shakespeare, two giants of the English literary canon, imitated regional accents in *The Reeve's Tale* and *King Lear* respectively, to poke fun at characters' social standing or regional background, and US author Mark Twain captured the voices of his protagonists using non-Standard English in books like *The Adventures of Huckleberry Finn* in the late nineteenth century, so this is not just a recent development.

For a long time, accents in southern England have been viewed as superior by many commentators and 'Good English' has often been seen as the preserve of the middle and upper classes of the south, especially those in London ... just so long as they were not Cockneys, of course, whose working class speech patterns were mercilessly mocked. Some of these attitudes have their roots in the gradual process of standardisation of English that you examined in Chapter 1, in which the importance of a recognised, official form of the language was seen as vital to reinforce the identity of England as a nation state and to facilitate clear communication between different groups of people within the nation. But as Hitchings points out, having a standard form of a language can be a two-edged sword:

> Standardization has general benefits, but often it has been practised not so much in the interests of the public at large as in those of the small

3 Attitudes to Language

authoritarian group who have enthroned their English as the best English. Yet, to flip things around, I could argue, as Thomas Sheridan did, that a standard form of English is a means of bringing about that great chimera, a classless society. In recent decades, this tension has been central to political debate about how English should be taught in schools: is the teaching of standard English a means of reinforcing the existing class structure, or does it offer children from less privileged backgrounds a passport to freedom? (Hitchings 2011a: 206–207)

Regional variation could therefore be seen as standing in the way of this standardisation, presenting an obstacle to those who wish to promote adherence to the 'chimera' Hitchings refers to (something that is wished for but almost impossible to achieve): a shared way of speaking and writing across the whole country. Indeed, some regional varieties have been viewed as old-fashioned and the speakers of them as educationally underdeveloped. As time has gone on and people's lives have changed, reflecting the more mobile and interconnected nature of our modern existence, more and more people have been exposed to different forms of English from around the UK and the world, leading to a gradual decline in the strength of regional and local dialects (a process called dialect levelling, which is covered in more detail in Chapter 1 of the Cambridge Topics in English Language series, *Language Diversity* book).

Of course, many people can speak more than one form of English. In reality, most people are adept at code-switching or style-shifting: moving between two forms of a language (or even two dialects or languages) in different situations. As Standard English is taught in all schools and the vast majority of printed material that we read is in this form, we all have access to it. That was not always the case, however, and there is an argument that speakers of regional dialects in centuries gone by might have been accurately viewed as uneducated, at least in terms of formal education.

KEY TERMS

Dialect levelling: the process by which language forms of different parts of the country converge and become more similar over time, with the loss of regional features and reduced diversity of language

Code-switching: speakers who speak two dialects of a language or two entirely different languages, switching from one to the other depending on whom they are talking to or what they wish to accomplish

Style-shifting: moving between different levels of formality or register in the same language

Attitudes to language variation

Additionally, it is difficult to unpick where regional variation ends and social variation begins. As the linguist Urszula Clark puts it on the pages of her project *West Midlands English: Speech and Society* (see www.cambridge.org/links/escatt6012):

> … speaking with a regional accent more likely indicated a working class background and state education for children, with various stereotypical characteristics assigned to differing regions. So, a West Country accent [from south-west England] would be associated with being a country bumpkin and lack of intelligence; a cockney accent [from east London] with slipperiness and deceit, a northern accent with being untrustworthy and a Birmingham or West Midlands accent [from central England] with stupidity.

3.2.1 Class and 'regionless' accents

As Standard English grew in status as the prestige dialect in the UK, certain accents also gained prominence at the expense of regional accents. Regional accents were often viewed as a mark of low social standing and so the middle classes were encouraged to send their children to private boarding schools to address this linguistic 'deficiency', as this letter from Elizabeth Montagu in 1773 reveals:

> I am glad you intend to send my eldest neice* to a boarding school. What girls learn at their schools is trifling, but they unlearn what could be of great disservice – a provincial accent, which is extremely ungenteel … I dare say you will find great improvement in her air and her speech by the time she has been there a year, and these are points of great importance. The Kentish dialect [from south-east England] is abominable, though not so bad as the Northumberland [from north-east England] and some others; but in this polished age, it is so unusual to meet with young ladies who have any patois, that I mightily wish to see my neice cured of it.

Note: neice* (original and non-standard spelling reproduced from original)

> **KEY TERM**
>
> **Patois:** the dialect of a particular group, especially one with low status in relation to the standard language

The accent that is probably most associated with prestige and tradition in the UK is Received Pronunciation (RP), which became established in the later nineteenth and early twentieth century, helped in no small part by the expansion of the middle class and the influence of private schools. As the nineteenth century drew to a close, the educated middle classes attending these schools – wherever they were in the UK – were taught to pronounce certain sounds in the same way,

Attitudes to Language

shaving the rough edges off the different accents that the students brought with them and developing a new accent that both identified them as members of a new elite and hid their original regional origins.

RP was helped by the BBC, which began its radio broadcasting in 1922 and employed presenters from quite a narrow and privileged social range, most (if not all) of whom spoke RP and were products of the same education and class system. This helped to establish RP as an aspirational model for those who listened and it was among this growing radio audience that RP gained its status and stranglehold on the nation's perceptions (and vowels).

> ### ACTIVITY 3.2
> Received Pronunciation
>
> Listen to the British Library's 'Sounds Familiar?' pages for some of the sounds of RP and more on its background: www.cambridge.org/links/escatt6001
>
> What are its distinctive characteristics? How does it differ to other accents that you might have heard in the UK and elsewhere?

3.2.2 Attitudes to RP

While RP is estimated to be spoken by only around 2 per cent of the UK population, it still commands a prestigious position in most surveys of attitudes to accents. When Howard Giles and Peter Powesland carried out their landmark 'matched guise' experiments in the 1970s, a script delivered in an RP accent to a group of school students was rated much higher for intelligence than exactly the same script delivered in a Birmingham accent to a similar group:

> The differences in the responses of each group were significant. The direct question about intelligence got answers showing that the lecturer was rated higher in his RP 'guise' than in his Birmingham one – in spite of the fact that he gave precisely the same talk, introduced himself as a university lecturer, and in every other way behaved in the same way to each group. Moreover, the students wrote far more both *to* him and *about* him in his RP than in his Birmingham guise (24 per cent more to him and 82 per cent more about him). Assuming that the groups of students who heard the two guises were reasonably similar in composition (and there is no reason to think otherwise), the explanation for these differences in *behaviour* between the two groups must have something to do with their attitudes to the two accents used. (Hudson 2004: 213)

Recent surveys of attitudes to accents by UK polling organisations such as ITV/ComRes (2013) and YouGov (2014) show RP as maintaining its prime position as an accent of education and intelligence (for example, see Table 3.1).

Attitudes to language variation

Table 3.1: Attitudes to accents (ITV/ComRes 2013)

	Very intelligent	Fairly intelligent	Neither intelligent nor unintelligent	Not very intelligent	Not all intelligent	Don't know	NET: Intelligent	NET: Unintelligent
Received Pronunciation/ Queen's English	31%	32%	27%	2%	1%	7%	62%	3%
Edinburgh	8%	30%	44%	7%	2%	9%	38%	9%
Devon	5%	23%	46%	12%	3%	10%	28%	15%
Belfast	4%	19%	48%	14%	5%	10%	23%	19%
Cardiff	4%	19%	52%	12%	4%	9%	23%	16%
Manchester	4%	16%	50%	17%	5%	8%	20%	22%
Newcastle	4%	15%	46%	19%	7%	9%	19%	26%
London (Cockney)	3%	14%	43%	25%	7%	7%	18%	32%
Birmingham	3%	12%	44%	22%	11%	8%	15%	33%
Liverpool	3%	12%	40%	24%	13%	8%	15%	37%

55

3 Attitudes to Language

On a less nuanced measure of approval (how 'attractive' each of 12 regional accents would be), the YouGov poll saw RP as second to Southern Irish (see Figure 3.2).

Figure 3.2: The most attractive accents in the British Isles, according to a YouGov poll in 2014

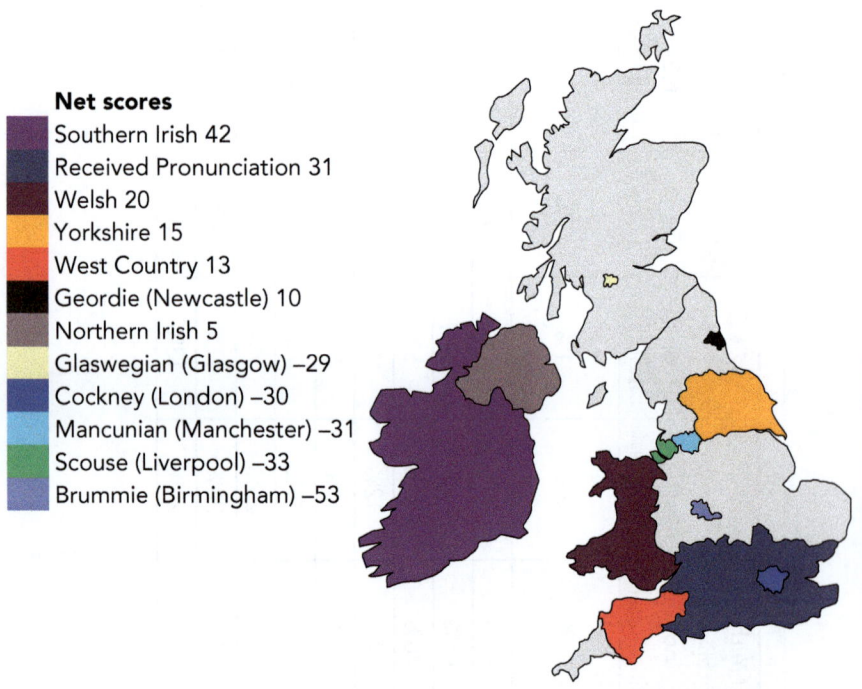

Net scores
Southern Irish 42
Received Pronunciation 31
Welsh 20
Yorkshire 15
West Country 13
Geordie (Newcastle) 10
Northern Irish 5
Glaswegian (Glasgow) –29
Cockney (London) –30
Mancunian (Manchester) –31
Scouse (Liverpool) –33
Brummie (Birmingham) –53

However, while RP is associated with education and intelligence, other surveys suggest that it is not viewed as favourably when it comes to warmth and friendliness. The ComRes poll that had RP as its most intelligent accent also had it as much lower for other qualities (see Table 3.2).

Attitudes to language variation

Table 3.2: The friendliest accents, according to ITV/ComRes (2013)

	Very friendly	Fairly friendly	Neither friendly nor unfriendly	Not very friendly	Not at all friendly	Don't know	NET: Friendly	NET: Unfriendly
Devon	21%	44%	24%	3%	1%	8%	65%	4%
Newcastle	19%	38%	26%	9%	4%	5%	56%	13%
Edinburgh	14%	38%	28%	11%	3%	5%	51%	15%
Cardiff	13%	38%	30%	9%	4%	6%	51%	13%
London (Cockney)	13%	36%	29%	14%	6%	3%	49%	19%
Liverpool	12%	31%	28%	16%	9%	4%	42%	26%
Belfast	10%	30%	29%	16%	8%	7%	41%	24%
Received Pronunciation/ Queen's English	11%	27%	35%	17%	7%	4%	38%	23%
Manchester	9%	29%	36%	17%	4%	5%	38%	21%
Birmingham	8%	28%	37%	15%	6%	5%	37%	21%

Attitudes to Language

This discrepancy between the two responses might indicate something about the nature of prestige accents, something that the linguists Mark Stewart, Ellen Bouchard Ryan and Howard Giles (1985) identified in what they refer to as 'status and solidarity'. In a study of American respondents' reactions to a range of accents, both American and British, the RP accent was viewed as having high status but low solidarity. In other words, the accent is respected but not particularly liked.

> **RESEARCH QUESTION**
> Researching attitudes to accents
>
> What are the main attitudes to different accents where you live? Do people in your area see the local accent (if there is a noticeable one) as something that is warm, friendly, intelligent or something to aspire to? Do others comment on your accent or that of your friends if you go somewhere else?
>
> Devise a methodology for measuring these attitudes and think about how you might account for variables such as the content of what people are saying, their gender and/or age. Think about the way in which you gather this data to give you a snapshot of attitudes to your local accent and others around the UK or world.
>
> Put together your findings as a mini-presentation, either to other students in your class or as a slideshow to present online.

3.2.3 Shifting up and down

These attitudes to RP might explain why some speakers of RP feel the need to converge downwards to a more working class accent or one that indicates fewer class origins, such as Estuary English: a variety of English identified by David Rosewarne in 1984 and described as such because its speakers tend to be located in outer London and the counties of Essex and Kent adjoining the estuary of the River Thames, as well as other parts of the south-east of England (see Figure 3.3).

Attitudes to language variation

Figure 3.3: Areas around the Thames Estuary in England

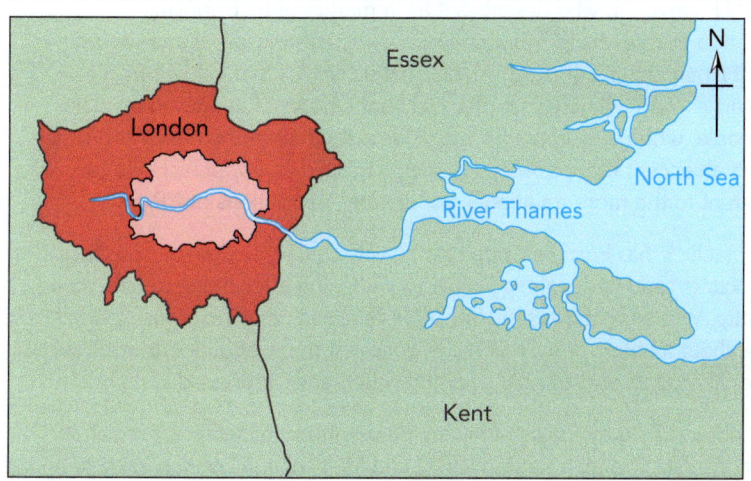

Convergence is part of what linguists term accommodation theory. This is a process through which speakers change their usual speech style (accent, level of formality, grammar, among other things) to either converge towards other speakers or diverge away from them. In the case of RP, the negative social connotations of the accent have led some politicians – former UK Prime Minister Tony Blair and former Chancellor of the Exchequer Gideon 'George' Osborne among them – to converge downwards to the perceived level of their working and/or middle class audiences and employ a less prestigious but more approachable linguistic style, often that of Estuary English.

KEY TERMS

Convergence: how speakers move speech styles and patterns to more closely match those of other speakers

Accommodation theory: how people adjust their speech behaviours to match others. This can be aspects of accent, grammar, vocabulary and even the style of speech delivery

Divergence: when an individual changes their language choices (usually temporarily) to become more dissimilar to another individual or group

3 Attitudes to Language

Estuary English has been described as a 'classless accent' by some, including Guðlaug Hilmarsdóttir, who describes it as 'a marker of metropolitan sophistication that seems to transcend previously existing social and linguistic barriers' (Hilmarsdóttir 2006: 4). An alternative view is that Estuary English actually carries with it its own set of social connotations. It is viewed by many young people, who have grown up with it as ubiquitous in the media and wider society, as an accent that projects a modern, relaxed and approachable persona: very different to the more traditional and starchy associations of RP.

Less charitably, it has been described as 'ghastly Estuary sludge' or 'mockney' (mock Cockney) and its speakers judged to be 'faking it' or trying to hide their real identity. Whatever the case – and linguists would recoil from such loaded language about features of speech – it is clear that many attitudes towards social and regional accents are strongly held and vehemently expressed.

And it is not just Estuary English that can be used to signal different social connotations. Black British English (BBE) and Multicultural London English (MLE) are both products of ethnic and social diversity in some of the UK's big cities and their use is not limited simply to members of ethnic minorities. You can read more about the links between language and ethnicity in the Cambridge book, *Language Diversity* (Clayton and Drummond, 2018), but (briefly) here you might also wish to consider how for many younger people, Black English (whether it is African-American English or BBE) and MLE are seen as having high prestige.

3.2.4 Internalised attitudes and social impact

This is an important part of the study of language because it reveals that others' attitudes towards varieties of English can lead us to internalise such views and make changes to our own language based on how we wish to be perceived. For example, if we are constantly told through comments on TV shows or in advertising campaigns that a certain accent is less accepted, or even an object of ridicule, we might avoid using this accent, even if it is one we would naturally speak in.

Interestingly, when judged by non-UK residents, the Birmingham accent ('Brummie') is not viewed as being ugly. As Steve Thorne notes:

> This strongly suggests that [British English speakers'] attitudes towards the dialect are influenced by factors such as social snobbery, negative media stereotyping, the poor public image of the city of Birmingham, and the north-south geographical and linguistic divide. (Thorne 2003)

Attitudes to language variation

On the flip side to this, the RP accent has become Hollywood's go-to voice for villains. As Chi Luu explains:

> … speakers of the prestige Received Pronunciation (RP) accent (otherwise known as the Queen's English or BBC English) are regularly evaluated by non-RP speakers as more educated, intelligent, competent, physically attractive, and generally of a higher socioeconomic class. At the same time, in terms of social attractiveness, those same posh RP speakers are consistently rated less trustworthy, kind, sincere, and friendly than speakers of non-RP accents. Sounds like a good start for a villain. (Luu 2017)

ACTIVITY 3.3
Accents in advertising

Read Text 3A, which is taken from *The Guardian*. Summarise the key findings about the respondents' attitudes to regional accents and identify the main issues around these attitudes. What factors influence how people might judge a particular accent?

Text 3A

> Locally accented ads work best in Newcastle and Manchester, but not in Birmingham and Bristol, according to government study
>
> Many people claim to hate the sound of their own voice, but a new government survey suggests the sensation is more unpleasant for some of us than it is for others. The study, commissioned by the Central Office of Information (COI), reveals that, while Geordies and Mancunians enjoy listening to their own regional accents in government advertisements, Brummies and Bristolians would rather not be subjected to their own distinctive burr.
>
> The COI [...] found responses to radio and TV commercials vary widely in different parts of the UK according to the accent they are recorded in. Residents of some regions, including Tyneside and Manchester, prefer to listen to government warnings about the dangers of drink driving or smoking cigarettes when they feature actors speaking in the local vernacular. Others, including those who live in the West Midlands and

3 Attitudes to Language

Bristol, are more likely to sit up and take notice when they are made using "received pronunciation", the COI study claims.

The survey [...] compared government messages recorded in local accents with identical adverts that used a generic "English" voice. It was designed to evaluate the effectiveness of government advertising, and assess whether it has more impact when filmed in regional dialects. In many parts of the country, the answer was a resounding "yes" – or "aye".

Tynesiders appear to be proud of their accents, [...] but Brummies responded negatively to hearing their vowels on TV and radio, partly because they recognise they are ridiculed for them by some of their compatriots.

"The research clearly shows that the accent used in radio and TV advertising can have an impact on how the ad is received," said Brian Jenkins, the head of radio at the COI. "Regional accents can make a difference but not necessarily a positive one. There was quite a negative reaction from people in Birmingham and Bristol to their own accents," he said. Jenkins added respondents in both cities were "very proud" of the way they spoke, but seem to have been affected by "other people's perceptions of their accent".

> 'Not all regions like to hear their own accents in ads, survey finds',
> Mark Sweney and James Robinson (*The Guardian*, 13 May 2009)

While the personal impact of many of these negative attitudes to language variation is high, there are wider social implications, as alluded to in Text 3A. Companies make judgements about employees' accents and often make employment decisions based on social stereotypes associated with those accents. The UK bank First Direct was reported to have based some of its call centres in Yorkshire in the north-east of England because of the perceived warmth and honesty of the Yorkshire accent. The Geordie (Newcastle) accent also attracted businesses to set up call centres in the north-east, leading to the area being viewed as the most popular place to set up a call centre in the UK, in a survey in 2008. On the negative side, the actor of the original Darth Vader in *Star Wars*, David Prowse, claims to have been overlooked for the voice part of his character because of his strong south-western (Bristolian) accent.

Vocal coaching is widespread in the UK, with some companies offering customers the chance to 'flatten' or 'reduce' their accent and achieve success as a result. An example of an advertisement for such a company is reproduced in Text 3B.

Attitudes to language variation

Text 3B

Accent Reduction and Pronunciation

The way we speak is a physical process governed by speech organs which can be trained or reprogrammed by working through a series of specific drills, including mouth positioning, intonation, breathing and listening exercises.

You will be helped to develop a clear, engaging English accent by learning how to recognise the differences between your mother tongue and the Standard English accent, otherwise known as Received Pronunciation or RP. The Accent Reduction course in Manchester is ideal for fluent non-native English speakers who wish to improve their English pronunciation and soften their accent, or who want to learn techniques to develop a more powerful and engaging voice.

- Do you pronounce some words incorrectly?
- Do you think your accent stops you from being taken seriously at work or from developing your career?
- Do you speak good English, but people often ask you to repeat yourself?
- Do people ask where you're from, even though you've lived in the UK for years?

ACTIVITY 3.4
Advertising accent reduction

Consider the pros and cons of accent reduction, as advertised by the company in Text 3B. What benefits might be gained from 'reducing' an accent in such a way? What might be the problems or issues with such an approach?

Accent prejudice is not just a problem in commercial businesses but has been noted in education as well. In some universities, academics with regional (i.e. non-RP or non-southern) accents have reported discrimination based purely on their accents. Katie Edwards (2014) carried out research in this area (having been treated unfairly because of her own South Yorkshire accent) and interviewed a number of academics about their experiences:

> The female academics used terms like 'humiliating', 'embarrassing' and good old fashioned 'bullying' to describe their experiences of having a regional accent in academia. Three complained that students would 'take the mickey' out of them in class. One had been advised to 'drop the accent'

3 Attitudes to Language

because she wouldn't be taken seriously as an academic and would find it more difficult to get a job because she didn't fit in.

She found this to be true and developed a dual accented persona: one for work and one using her authentic accent, when she was around family and friends.

All the men I interviewed, although faced with similar experiences, purposefully maintained their accents, some becoming even broader in the face of ridicule.

In 2016, campaigners used the hashtag *#accentism* to draw attention to accent discrimination in academia and to highlight the social stereotyping inherent in such prejudices about certain regional accents.

3.2.5 Variation and education

Schools in the UK have also been involved in the debate about Standard and non-Standard English. While it is expected (and widely accepted) that all students will learn Standard English (and Standard American English and Standard Australian English in their respective countries) for clear, formal, written communication, very few people actually speak in the prestige dialect. To what extent should schools attempt to influence the language their students use when they are speaking in the classroom, canteen or playground?

Two schools in the UK that have been featured in the national press for their attempts to regulate their students' use of non-Standard English are Sacred Heart Primary in Teesside and Colley Lane in the area of the West Midlands known as the Black Country. Both schools issued letters to their students, asking parents to work with the schools to change students' speech habits. The head teacher of Colley Lane argued that he and the school valued the culture of the area and its distinct language identity but that they wanted 'to give our children the spoken language skills to compete against the best'.

> **ACTIVITY 3.5**
> School speech
> Read Text 3C, which reports on the attempts by Colley Lane school to regulate its students' use of language. Identify the key reasons the school gave for their campaign and the arguments against its approach.

Text 3C

Youngsters at a West Midlands primary school have been told "yow cor spaek lyuke that" by teachers fed-up with their regional 'slanguage'. Kids

Attitudes to language variation

are banned from saying Black Country phrases including "it wor me", "I day", "I cor do that", "gonna" and "woz" in classes.

Teachers at Colley Lane Primary School in Halesowen sent a 'Mind Your Slanguage' guide to stunned parents last week. They listed ten phrases and words now banned from the classroom, playground and corridors in a bid to improve language skills. Other phrases include "they was", "ya" instead of "you", "I ain't", "somefink" and "ay?" instead of "pardon".

Teachers said the "zero-tolerance" policy had been introduced because the regional phrases were "damaging" to pupils. In the letter, they claimed the harsh crackdown would "get children out of the habit" of speaking the way their parents do. It stated: "We asked each class teacher to write a list of the top ten most damaging phrases used by children in the classroom. We are introducing a 'zero tolerance' in the classroom to get children out of the habit of using the phrases on the list. We want the children to have the best start possible: Understanding when it is and is not acceptable to use slang and colloquial language. We value the local dialect but are encouraging children to learn the skill of turning it on and off in different situations."

But many parents reacted angrily to the move – accusing teachers of "de-Black Countrying" their kids. Alana Willetts, 30, whose nine-year-old son George attends the school, said: "I do not agree with this zero tolerance policy. The teachers should be teaching the children about the Black Country and our dialect. There are a lot of children who have no idea about local history. Some of my friends have gone on to be doctors and lawyers, I'm an engineer. It doesn't affect you as a person. I think it is patronising and insulting to say that people with a Black Country accent are disadvantaged. I have not been disadvantaged and there are plenty of people who are very successful. Many pop stars and other celebrities seem to have done well for themselves with a Black Country accent. All the parents are outraged, English is a living language, we can't all talk the same. We don't all speak in ye olde English and new words are being added to the dictionary every day."

Self-styled 'Black Country champion' Ryan Guest described the school ban as "ridiculous". He said: "Yes there's occasions where you have to speak in a more formal manner, but that just comes naturally as you grow older. Banning colloquialisms that come naturally to you as a person is just stupid and comes across as being quite snobbish. It hasn't done the likes of Lenny Henry or Noddy Holder too much harm, has it? Everybody should be proud of their roots and of their background. The Black Country accent and dialect is a key part of local people's identity."

Headteacher John White defended the school's anti-Black Country phrase policy. He said: "We talked about this a lot before we went ahead with the

3 Attitudes to Language

> policy. Children can get confused when it comes to the classroom about what is the right term to use. We wanted to do it in a light-hearted way and not be patronising. We value the Black Country heritage and that is important to us as a school. It is all about getting these children ready for that job interview when they can hold their own with people from across the country. How they speak with their mates is of course a different matter."
>
> Earlier this year a study was published claiming West Midlands accents make people seem less intelligent and untrustworthy.
>
>> 'Yow cor spaek lyuke that! West Midlands school bans pupils from using "damaging" regional slang', Martin Fricker (*Mirror*, 14 November 2013)

Along with the responses from parents, students and readers of local newspapers in these areas, linguists have taken some of these schools to task. While the desire to improve students' literacy is universally applauded, the methods used to achieve it are not necessarily approved of. Writing in *The Independent*, the linguist Julia Snell comments:

> Ultimately, it is not the presence or absence of non-standard forms in children's speech that raise educational issues; rather, picking on non-standard voices risks marginalising some children, and may make them less confident at school. Silencing pupils' voices, even with the best intentions, is just not acceptable. (Snell 2013)

Rob Drummond argues a similar point and suggests that more could be learnt from studying the non-standard language than banning it:

> ... banning slang in schools is a short-sighted and inefficient way of trying to produce young people who are confident and adaptable communicators. What we should be doing is encouraging students to explore the fluidity, richness, and contextual appropriateness of an ever-changing language. (Drummond, 2016)

At the heart of this debate are two distinct functions of language: the transactional function that is all about conveying ideas and information clearly from one person to another, and the interpersonal function that is more to do with language acting as a marker of identity and belonging. In these debates about Standard English in schools, the two functions are seen as being mutually antagonistic, when in fact they could be viewed as two sides of the same coin. The other assumption that seems to underlie these attempts to ban certain forms of English is that young people only have access to one form and cannot shift between styles. This runs contrary to what most linguistic research suggests.

Code-switching (moving between two languages or dialects) and style shifting (moving between different levels of formality or register) are linguistic realities for most people. All of us shape our language depending on our audience and

Attitudes to language variation

context and there is very little (if any) research to suggest that clamping down on non-Standard English has any positive effect on increasing young people's literacy ability. In fact, many linguists argue that by making young people feel more self-conscious of the 'flaws' in their regional dialect, there is a risk that their schools will put them at odds with their home environments, that they may not be willing to talk at all and therefore have opportunities denied to them. Others (including Honey 1989) have argued that both regional accents and non-Standard English hold back young people from educational and social progress.

3.3 Attitudes to other varieties

English exists in many forms around the world and is arguably the most popular in the world to learn as a second or additional language. One way of viewing this is to see English spreading out from England, but this presupposes that it has been a steady and gradual process and doesn't always acknowledge the individual identities of the new varieties. Perhaps a more suitable metaphor is that English is like a plant that has grown in the UK. The new varieties are cuttings from the original plant that have been picked up and transported to numerous countries around the world where they have taken on a life of their own and sometimes moved in quite different directions compared to the language spoken in the UK itself.

In fact, some would argue that the relationship between UK English and other world Englishes is now so distant as to mean that England no longer has any real influence on the language that takes its name. As one witty (but anonymous) online commentator put it, 'The English ... have as much control over English as the Italians have over pizza and Indians over chicken korma'.

However, not everyone is quite as relaxed about it. Some commentators complain that the different varieties of English spoken around the world are sub-standard versions of the 'real thing' and that UK English should still exert itself as a standard for others to emulate. This is a very similar argument to the one you have explored earlier in this chapter and elsewhere about the relationship between Standard English and non-standard varieties of it. As you can read in more detail in Chapter 4 of the CUP book on *Language Diversity* (Clayton and Drummond, 2018), world Englishes are not inferior versions of UK English, but developing and thriving forms of a living language.

Perhaps controversially, some (including the linguist Mario Saraceni, quoted here) have argued that 'the psychological umbilical cord' between England and world Englishes should be cut 'and people wherever they are – India, Malaysia, the USA or England – can do what they want with the language. Practically speaking, what does this mean? At the most basic level, it means that the books that English is taught from should get rid of their pictures of "red double-decker buses or post-boxes"'. (Saraceni 2008: 20–26)

3 Attitudes to Language

In many cases the English that has sprung up in new places has returned to the UK, either with people emigrating to the British Isles (from the Caribbean, West Africa, India and Australia, for example) or with world English varieties reaching us through online communication and global media (American English through Hollywood, Indian English through Bollywood and African-American English through hip hop, for example).

3.3.1 Attitudes to American English

One of the oldest varieties of English outside the UK is American English. Having been exported to the USA in the seventeenth century, American English has developed along its own path and become probably the most dominant form of English in the world, arguably surpassing the power of UK English.

Complaints in the UK about American English are not new. Like their populations, American and UK English had been living separate (if parallel) lives for much of their existence. American English gained its own spelling dictionary in the form of Noah Webster's 'Blue-Backed Speller' in 1787 and its own *American Dictionary of the English Language* in 1828 from Webster again. It was clear by this point that the two branches of English had some different vocabulary, spellings, grammar and word meanings.

David Marsh describes some of these changes and attitudes to them:

> As the two countries diverged, Americans retained some traditional usages that Britons lost, and vice versa. British English used to spell *cheque* 'check', as American English still does. You'd think purists would be pleased to see such respect for tradition, but no. They moan about the past participle gotten, which is standard in Scotland as well as the US, a remnant of Old English that survives in *ill-gotten gains*, *misbegotten*, *woebegotten*, and of course *forgotten*. (Marsh 2013: 200)

Complaints about American English use in the UK have often taken the form of arguments that English has its own perfectly good language and doesn't need to take imports from abroad, but underlying this are many of the wider social attitudes and prejudices that we have seen underpinning complaints about native forms of non-Standard English. Prince Charles, speaking in 1995 to a British Council audience, bemoaned what he saw as the 'very corrupting' influence of American English and stated that 'people tend to invent all sorts of nouns and verbs and make words that shouldn't be'. More recently, the journalist Matthew Engel has complained that:

> … nowadays, people have no idea where American ends and English begins. And that's a disaster for our national self-esteem. We are in danger of subordinating our language to someone else's – and with it large aspects of British life. (Engel 2010)

Attitudes to language variation

While attitudes to non-Standard English in the UK are often characterised by judgements about social background and class, those about American English can also add xenophobia and discourses of invasion. Marsh quotes a correspondent to *The Guardian* newspaper:

> Your journalists are increasingly using ugly Americanisms, presumably in the belief that it is 'edgy' and trendy to do so. Recent examples include pony up, mojo, sledding, duke it out, brownstones and suck, many of which are quite meaningless to me... I am not anti-American, but I do not see why our language should be corrupted by sloppy writing, and why there should be so much emphasis on all things American. (Marsh 2013: 199)

ACTIVITY 3.6
American English arguments

Read Text 3D, which is taken from Matthew Engel's article about American English. Also use this link to read a second article by Engel on the same topic: www.cambridge.org/links/escatt6002

Consider the arguments and opinions Engel puts forward and make a note of the examples he uses. Once you have read this, use the links to Lynne Murphy's blog post and Mark Liberman's response to Engel's views to explore the more nuanced and well-researched arguments put forward by linguists as to why Engel is so misguided.

The alternative views of Mark Liberman and Lynne Murphy can be found in these links:

- 'Peeve of the week: 20% correct': www.cambridge.org/links/escatt6003

- 'Anti-Americanismism Part 1': www.cambridge.org/links/escatt6004

Text 3D

> Sometimes, the language can be improved by the imports. The British would never be able even to define the deficit had we not adopted the American billion (a thousand million) to replace our old hardly used billion (a million million).
>
> I accept that estate agents find it easier to sell fancy apartments rather than boring old flats. And it's right that our few non-passenger trains should carry freight not goods, because that's a more accurate description of the contents.

3 Attitudes to Language

But the process is non-selective and almost wholly one-way. And it works very strangely. Almost all the parts of a car have different names in America, yet there is no sign of hood replacing bonnet, or the trunk supplanting the boot.

Meanwhile, the most improbable areas of activity are terminally infected. Take the law. Ask any lawyer and they will explain: witnesses in British courts do not testify, they give evidence; nor do they 'take the stand' to do this, they go into the witness box. They do things the American way in media reports of court cases, though – day after day.

We are witnessing a transatlantic takeover in politics as well. This month, Britain acquired a National Security Council. Last year, it gained a Supreme Court. There is talk that the House of Lords will be renamed the Senate.

It also used to be understood that, while American politicians 'ran' for office, British politicians always 'stood'. I liked that: it implied a pleasing reticence. Now in Britain both words are used interchangeably and in this month's General Election candidates stood and ran at the same time. No wonder they kept falling flat on their faces.

Then take sport, where Britain's national tastes are totally different from those of the Americans. I happen to belong to the .0001 per cent (approx) of the British population who count as baseball fans. This makes it even more offensive to me when politicians parrot phrases such as 'three strikes and you're out' although they haven't got the foggiest idea what it means.

Technical baseball terms are everywhere. We constantly hear about people 'stepping up to the plate'. For some weird reason, cricket coaches are especially fond of this one. And ideas keep coming from the baseball position of 'left field'. Wouldn't silly mid-on be more appropriate?

And so, hi guys, hel-LO, wake up and smell the coffee. We need to distinguish between the normal give-and-take of linguistic development and being overrun – through our own negligence and ignorance – by rampant cultural imperialism.

From 'Say no to the get-go! Americanisms swamping English, so wake up and smell the coffee', Mathew Engel (*Daily Mail*, 29 May 2010)

Given the close relationship between UK and US English, it should come as no surprise to see British English words entering the American English lexicon, a process called 'Anglocreep'. Words like 'ginger' (used to describe a person with red hair) or 'mate' (to describe a friend) have cropped up in American usage and caused consternation for some American commentators and delight among others.

Linguist Ben Yagoda has a website called *Not One-Off Britishisms* (www.cambridge.org/links/escatt6008), which traces such lexical developments, while linguist Lynne Murphy's *Separated by a Common Language* blog has also looked at this two-way relationship (www.cambridge.org/links/escatt6009).

> **PRACTICE QUESTION**
> Is American English a threat to other languages?
>
> Using the articles and resources in this section, along with your own ideas, plan and write an answer to the following exam-style question: 'American English is a threat to other language around the world, including English itself. What do you think of this idea and what evidence can you offer to support your argument?'
>
> Make sure you include references to the views of linguists, as well as those who have offered opinions and views on the issue in the media.

Opinions about language diversity are almost as varied as the varieties themselves. This is to be expected when language does so much more than just communicate ideas from one person to another. Language is also about identity, history, culture and a sense of belonging, so bound up with very personal feelings about who we are and where we fit into the world. When exploring attitudes to diversity it is important to remember this.

Wider reading

You can find out more about attitudes to language variation by reading the following:

Hitchings, H. (2011) *The Language Wars: A History of Proper English*. London: John Murray.

Kerswill, P. (2012) 'Language Variation 1' (2012: 23–43). In D. Clayton with English & Media Centre (ed.) *Language: A Student Handbook of Key Topics and Theories*. London: EMC.

Mencken, H.L. (2017) *The American Language: A Preliminary Inquiry Into the Development of English in the United States* (Classic Reprint – a modern reprint of the 1919 original).

Milroy, J. and Milroy, L. (1985) *Authority in Language: Investigating Standard English*. London: Routledge.

3 Attitudes to Language

Watson, K. (2012: 44–59) 'Language Variation 2'. In D. Clayton with English & Media Centre (ed.) *Language: A Student Handbook of Key Topics and Theories*. London: EMC.

Linguists and commentators have responded in a number of ways to campaigns against local and regional dialect being banned in schools, and you can read more from the following link: http://englishlangsfx.blogspot.co.uk/2013/02/driving-up-standards-by-driving-out-non.html

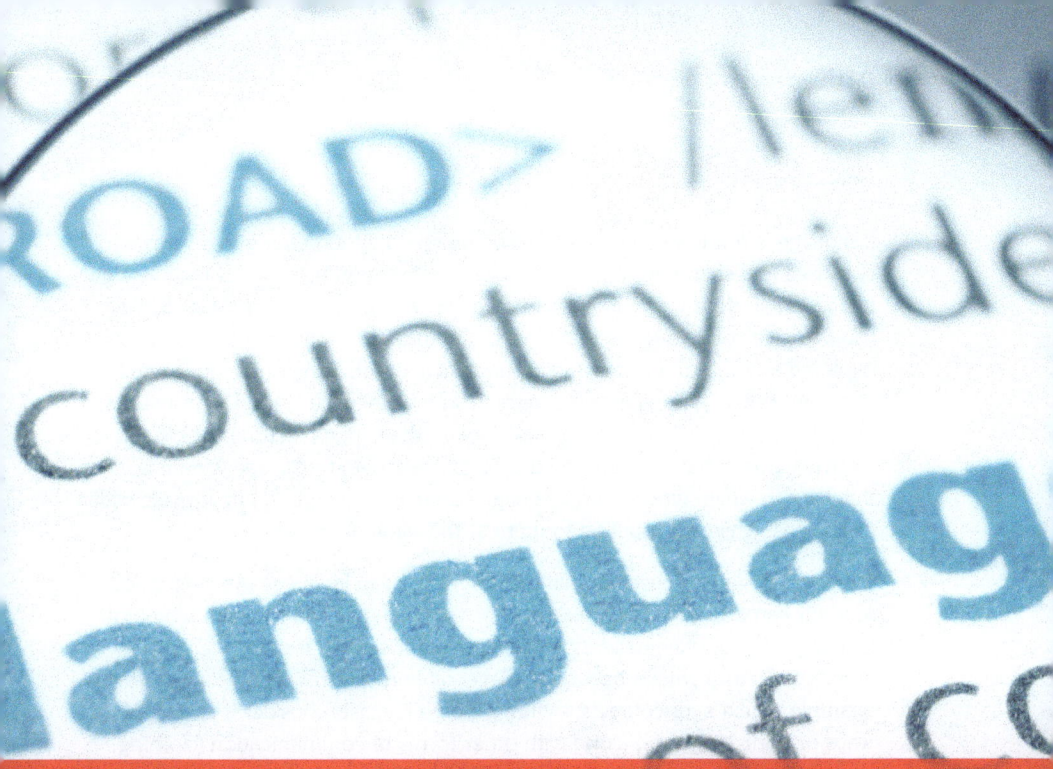

Chapter 4
Language discourses

In this chapter you will:

- Study the idea of discourses around language use
- Develop a 'toolkit' to analyse texts about language
- Apply your understanding to short text extracts and whole texts

4 Attitudes to Language

4.1 Analysing language discourses

Language is not just something that we discuss: it is something that we use to construct and shape arguments and ideas with. Different forms of language give rise to very different opinions and views, but we also use language in different ways to give voice to these attitudes. In the three previous chapters, you have explored a range of debates and arguments about the English language and in this chapter you will explore the ways in which language is used to frame those attitudes. As part of this you will also look at the various recurrent themes and 'conversations' that exist around language change and language variation, and the ways in which writers and language commentators often mirror these wider discourses, while contributing to them at the same time.

'Discourse' is a term used in many different ways in language and linguistics, and this can cause some confusion. The term can be used to mean a type of language (e.g. spoken or written discourse) or it can be used to refer to how a text works as a whole, beyond the level of words, phrases and clauses (for example, a text's 'discourse structure'). Some linguists consider it as one of the ways of using language, along with other forms of communication (clothing, body language, etc.), that signals your membership of a social group or network.

Here, the term is being used in a way that is probably more influenced by its meaning in the social sciences and sociolinguistics, as ways of thinking about, talking about, arguing about and describing how we feel about language. Discourses are like conversations that take place about topics and a discourse might often follow a particular pattern, where familiar arguments crop up time and again.

Discourses are important because they can help to frame the way we think about the world. The linguist Norman Fairclough (1989: 14), who was one of the first to pioneer what has become known as Critical Discourse Analysis (CDA) argues that '… language is centrally involved in power, and struggles for power…' and that 'Ideologies are closely linked to language, because using language is the commonest form of social behaviour, and the form of social behaviour where we rely most on "common-sense" assumptions'.

> **KEY TERM**
>
> **Critical Discourse Analysis:** an approach to the study of both written and spoken language focusing on the ways that power is enacted

Language can influence the way we interpret the world around us and our place in it, so it is important to ask questions about the ways in which language helps construct ideas and to challenge those ideas with linguistic analysis.

Language discourses

As Fairclough explains, language is a particularly powerful tool in the battle for power because it is so ubiquitous. It encodes nearly all of our experiences and interactions, and helps construct the reality that we live in. But the fact that it is all around us all the time often blinds us to the fact that everyday language can actually describe things, events, people and processes in ways that we accept without thinking. Think about the following fairly common English expressions and sayings, and consider how they create a particular view of the world:

- I've been feeling really down.
- His argument went down a blind alley.
- The debate began to heat up.
- The video has gone viral.

The notion that happiness is 'up' and sadness 'down' is one that is firmly established in English and one that many of us would take for granted, as is the idea of excitement and vigour as hot while being calm and distant would be seen as cold. The phrase 'blind alley' is a metaphor for a dead end but 'blind' itself is metaphorical, again easily understood. The representation of the spread of a video online as being viral again takes a term from one area (medicine) and transfers it to a different field (media). Interestingly, all of these are metaphors in which one process or phenomenon is described in the terms of something else, and this is an aspect of discourse analysis that you will look at as this chapter progresses.

4.2 Describing language

In Chapter 1, you looked at an extract from an article by Lindsay Johns, complaining about the 'ghetto grammar' used by many young people and how he sees it as an obstacle to employment and education. We will study the whole article later in this chapter, along with several other examples of writing about language, but here we can look at one particular section of the article to illustrate the points above.

Text 4A

> The English language is an incredibly rich inheritance. Yet it is being squandered by so many young people of all races and backgrounds.
>
> Extract from 'Ghetto grammar robs the young of a proper voice', Lindsay Johns (*Evening Standard*, 16 August 2011)

4 Attitudes to Language

When Johns describes English as 'an incredibly rich inheritance', he is representing the language in one particular way and by using one particular metaphor. An inheritance is usually something (and it is usually a 'thing') that is passed down from one generation to the next. By premodifying this noun with the adjective phrase 'incredibly rich', he magnifies the importance and financial connotations of this thing. But is language really a thing to be passed down like an object? In one way it could be, because as we have seen, language is something that we all contribute to and it is heavily influenced by those around it. But to describe it as an inheritance is perhaps to describe it as a thing that is passed down unchanged and intact from generation to generation.

Is language like that? Not really. It changes as time goes on and its shape is altered to match the needs of its users. By using the noun 'inheritance', the writer is tapping into a familiar discourse around language, that of tradition and heritage. And by casting language as something that he explains is 'being squandered' he again places it in the position of an object: grammatically, he is using the passive voice here and showing that language ('it') is having forces act upon it. In grammatical terms, the passive shows that the subject of the sentence is receiving the action of the verb. The value of language in the first sentence is contrasted with the casual lack of attention to its worth in the second and a discourse of decline and degeneration is perhaps evident.

On their own, these two sentences are not enough to offer a full discussion of the text, but the fact that Johns has tapped into an already existing way of thinking about language – a discourse that language has value but is being wasted by the young – allows him to show that his view has a context and a backdrop that can be easily recognised by his readers. It is in this way that language discourses often work. Pre-existing conversations and opinions about language form a thread and, over time, these build up into a view that many people start to see as the accepted norm. A 'common-sense' view that language is changing, and not for the better, establishes itself and becomes hard to shake off. The linguist John McWhorter suggests in the introduction to *Words on the Move* (2016: 1) that 'if polled, few of us would put a check next to the statement "I think language should never change". However, so often we don't like it when the change actually happens. Somehow it seems that language is always changing in the *wrong* ways'.

When it comes to analysing language discourses you need to be aware of the ways in which language itself is represented and to consider how these representations are created and what they might reveal. In this chapter, you will revisit some of the topic areas from the previous chapters – language change, technology and language variation – looking closely at how ideas about language are constructed and how language analysis can be used to peel away the different layers of meaning and reveal different ideological positions.

Language discourses

4.2.1 Discourses

Opinions about language can range across the spectrum, from deep disquiet about how language is changing and how it varies from person to person through to a happy acceptance of the inevitability of change and embracing of diversity. Sometimes, these opinions are laid out in stark, straightforward terms, with writers being quite clear in telling readers exactly what their approach is (for example, 'As a prescriptivist, I believe that language change must be stopped'). On other occasions, attitudes are expressed using a range of different devices: metaphors, similes, analogies and extended metaphors, often describing language in terms of something else: a building, a tide, a disease, a combatant in a battle or an animal. These all contribute towards the creation of different discourses: ways of thinking about, talking about, arguing about and describing how we feel about language, as explained earlier in this chapter.

These discourses often help to shape a particular viewpoint about the topic and perhaps close down other ways of viewing the issue. For example, if language is represented as a place of conflict between two forces – good and evil – it leaves little room to consider alternative models: that language change is not a series of conflicts but a constant process of gradual change or that language is neither good nor bad but a neutral and amoral process. If language change is represented using a discourse of disease and infection, its spread is portrayed as harmful and damaging, and those who spread it as dangerous.

ACTIVITY 4.1

Diagnosing discourses

Read Text 4B, Text 4C and Text 4D. Each is taken, or adapted, from an article about language. What discourses are presented to the readers and what do they tell us about the views being offered by each writer? What alternative viewpoints might you offer?

Text 4B

> It is the relentless onward march of the texters, the SMS (Short Message Service) vandals who are doing to our language what Genghis Khan did to his neighbours eight hundred years ago. They are destroying it: pillaging our punctuation; savaging our sentences; raping our vocabulary. And they must be stopped. This, I grant you, is a tall order. The texters have many more arrows in their quiver than we who defend the old way.
>
> Extract from 'I h8 text msgs: How texting is wrecking our language', John Humphrys (*Daily Mail*, 24 September 2007)

4 Attitudes to Language

Text 4C

> English has prospered through assimilating terms from other languages, and engagement – in London and beyond – with speakers of foreign languages has enabled this, while also propagating hybrids such as Hinglish (a blend of Hindi and English). London English has long been wildly diverse. In the 14th century, Geoffrey Chaucer absorbed words of French and Italian origin; recycling them was a way to make his writing appear more dignified. Today the multiplicity of tongues on our streets means scope for cross-pollination is much greater.
>
> Extract from 'Language can't stay still – just listen to London', Henry Hitchings (*Evening Standard*, 1 February 2011)

Text 4D

> ... the rise of texting is creating a generation of young people whose standards for the basic tools of communication – spelling, grammar, sentence structure, all that good stuff – are rapidly decreasing.
>
> As a space apparently without rules and regulations, it seems as though literacy standards would instantly dissolve on the Internet. Text messaging also seems a likely candidate for the decline of the English language, since the physical constraints of a phone's keyboard make brevity a bonus, often via unconventional spelling.
>
> If any technological advancement is warping our children's ability to spell, the argument goes, it must be text messaging.
>
> Extract from 'English can absorb assault from texting', Shannon Corregan (*Times Colonist*, 9 March 2012)

From the extracts you can probably see a number of different representations of language change and diversity. Language is represented using discourses of invasion, conflict and decline, along with metaphors of movement and nature. A range of different discourses around language can be found across many texts. A few of these are outlined below:

- **Correctness:** language is seen as being either right or wrong, correct or incorrect.

- **Morality:** language use is seen as being good or bad and its users as good or bad people.

- **Conflict:** arguments about language are framed as being about two sides in opposition.

- **Decline:** language is represented as a once great thing that is undergoing a steady decline from its peak in the past.

- **Pollution:** language is represented as something pure but at risk of pollution.
- **Infection and disease:** change or variation is seen as a threat to the health of the language, weakening and damaging it.
- **Invasion:** language is seen as under threat from outside forces.

> **RESEARCH QUESTION**
> Researching language discourses
>
> Using the texts that you gathered from the research task at the start of Chapter 1, identify the different discourses being used to describe some of the issues around language change and variation. Classify the different discourses using the suggested list and try to identify other discourses that might be relevant.
>
> You can use this data set to set up some research questions for a 'Language investigation' suggested at the end of this chapter.

4.3 A language toolkit

To get to grips with arguments and debates about language, it is important to have the ability to analyse the language in detail. To do this, you will need a language toolkit. Different levels of analysis are required to unlock the meanings and representations created through language, including grammar, semantics and pragmatics. However, alongside them, it is important to understand patterns and structures across whole texts and groups of texts. The language itself though cannot be separate from the creator of it and this is where ideas such as positioning and address become extremely important. Discourses about language do not just appear out of thin air: they are created and shaped by writers of texts who put forward views and offer their own perspectives.

When analysing language discourses, a three-pronged focus can be employed, drawing on the ideas of linguist Michael Halliday and systemic functional linguistics. According to Halliday, language has three main functions: ideational, interpersonal and textual.

- **Ideational function:** used to represent experiences and convey a version of reality.
- **Interpersonal function:** used to represent the nature of relationships between writers of texts and their audiences, along with the positions adopted by the writers in relation to their audiences.
- **Textual function:** used to organise and structure language material into a coherent whole.

4 Attitudes to Language

While some discourses are presented using fairly simple similes (e.g. 'The English language is collapsing like a ruined building in front of our very eyes'), which are instantly recognisable with little detailed grasp of language analysis, other more subtle aspects of meaning can be discerned with a wider range of methods. In the example above, look at how grammar is used in a number of ways:

- The present tense ('is') and progressive aspect ('collapsing') are employed to create a sense of ongoing action taking place at this very moment, perhaps in order to accentuate the severity of this process. (Ideational function)

- The declarative mood is used in the simple sentence to present a statement as a simple fact. There is no sense of doubt or possibility here, which might have come from the use of a modal verb ('*might* be seen as…') or modal adverb ('perhaps'). (Interpersonal and ideational functions)

- The preposition phrase ('in front of our very eyes') uses the first person plural pronoun/possessive determiner *our* to create a sense of shared viewpoint. (Interpersonal function)

- This extract might form part of a wider discourse about language falling apart, linking it to several other similar devices as part of a coherent argument put forward by the writer. (Textual function)

So, along with the simile, a number of other devices amplify the particular viewpoint being put forward, perhaps making it appear more convincing.

The kinds of language tools that are useful for this kind of analysis can vary, but the following are discussed below:

- noun phrases and modification
- verb phrases and modality
- pronouns and address
- patterns.

For more detailed discussion about some of these, the Cambridge Topics in English Language series *Text Analysis and Representation* by Ian Cushing and *The Language of Literature: An Introduction to Stylistics* by Marcello Giovanelli and Jessica Mason are recommended.

4.3.1 Noun phrases and modification

Noun phrases are groups of words centred on a head word that is a noun. When analysing texts about language, noun phrases can be a useful starting point, because they will invariably be used to represent the topic in a way that creates a particular view. The example quoted in Chapter 1 from Lindsay Johns' 'Ghetto Grammar' article (2011) is a case in point. In the sentence, 'The English language is an incredibly rich inheritance', the noun phrase 'an incredibly rich inheritance' is used as the complement in the clause to describe the English language. The noun phrase consists of a determiner, adverb and adjective, which are used to modify and describe the noun 'inheritance'.

While 'inheritance' is a strong noun in its own right, with connotations of wealth and tradition, the adjective that modifies it ('rich') accentuates these qualities and the adverb intensifying the adjective ('incredibly') adds to this. The determiner may or may not be interesting, but the fact that it is an indefinite article ('an') rather than a definite article ('the') might suggest that there are other inheritances, of which the language is just one. In the subsequent sentence, 'Yet it is being squandered....', the pronoun *it* functions as a noun phrase itself and refers back to the noun phrase in the previous sentence. In this way, the concept of what the English language is has already been established and the pronoun now takes on the role of signalling that idea, packaging it up in a way that takes it as a given.

4.3.2 Verb phrases and modality

Verb phrases are groups of verbs working together as a unit. While noun phrases tend to describe objects, people and ideas, verb phrases describe processes, states of being and actions. These are useful to explore when analysing language discourses because the combination of certain verbs can create a number of different meanings.

Tense and aspect are two such features. In the second sentence above, the verb phrase '... is being squandered' makes use of the present tense auxiliary verb ('is') and the progressive auxiliary verb ('being') to work alongside the main verb in the participle form ('squandered') to indicate that the action is ongoing and taking place contemporaneously. Perhaps the implication of this is that if it is happening now, something can be done to stop the process. Had it been a completed action, no such chance would exist.

> ### KEY TERMS
> **Tense:** how language indicates when an event or action took place. In English, this is usually defined as past or present (and there is some debate over whether English has a genuine future tense)
>
> **Aspect:** how language indicates whether an action or event is or has been completed or ongoing; in English, this is usually separated into perfective or progressive.

Another element of the sentence above is the use of the passive voice. In this case, the action of the verb phrase is being carried out against the subject of the

Attitudes to Language

sentence ('it' – the pronoun referring back to 'The English language' from the previous sentence). The passive voice allows the writer to show that the subject of the sentence is having actions carried out against it, being acted upon, rather than having agency over its own verb processes.

> **ACTIVITY 4.2**
> Verb phrases
>
> Study each of the following examples and decide how the active or passive voice and the use of tense and aspect might work to shape meaning.
>
> - The language is being invaded by Americanisms.
> - Slang and textisms are infiltrating the language of young people.
> - English has been suffering a gradual decline.

Modal auxiliary verbs can work alongside other verbs to affect meanings in clauses and represent ideas about language in many ways. The nine modal auxiliary verbs in English (*can, may, shall, will, could, would, should, would* and *must*) work alongside main verbs to affect the meaning of them. Modals often increase the level of certainty or doubt connected to a main verb or exert some kind of force on it. Modal verbs are also important because they help to express a stance on the part of the person who is using them.

> **KEY TERM**
>
> **Modal auxiliary verb:** a modal auxiliary is a verb that works alongside other verbs to express degrees of certainty, obligation, possibility and permission.

When John Humphrys (2007) expresses his distaste for texting and those who use it, describing them as 'vandals who are doing to our language what Genghis Khan did to his neighbours eight hundred years ago … destroying it: pillaging our punctuation; savaging our sentences; raping our vocabulary', he completes his paragraph with the line, 'And they must be stopped.' The modal *must* implies a degree of force and a clear position on Humphrys' part: strong opposition to the (admittedly hyperbolic) onward march of the texters. It acts as a call to arms in his campaign to oppose texting and its effects on language. The modal is inserted as part of his attempt to position himself (and, hopefully, his readers) as a force in opposition to the invading horde and this discourse of combat and invasion is magnified by his language choices.

Elsewhere, modal verbs can be used to do other jobs:

- to prescribe ways of using language, e.g. 'the split infinitive *should* be avoided'
- to suggest potential or capability, e.g. 'we *can* all stand against this invasion of our language'
- to suggest future possibility, e.g. 'one day, we *might* see emojis replace words'.

4.3.3 Pronouns and address

Another way in which the interpersonal function can be used is through pronouns. When writers use personal pronouns, they reveal something of the stance they wish to take in relation to the topic they are writing about and the readers they would like to address. A simple example is the use of the second-person pronoun *you*, which can often be used to address a reader directly, creating a sense (if only an artificial one, in many cases) of interaction and engagement.

Addressing a reader as if they are known to the writer is known as synthetic personalisation: an artificial relationship is constructed between text producer and text receiver, often with the aim of bridging the gap between writer and reader that exists in a written text where the nature of the actual reader is unknown to the person doing the writing.

KEY TERM

Synthetic personalisation: a technique identified by the linguist Norman Fairclough in which an audience is addressed in a way that suggests they are known as individuals

Similarly, using first-person plural pronouns (*we* and *us*) or a possessive determiner (*our*) helps to position a text producer alongside or among the ideal readers. Think about how pronouns are used in the following examples to help position the writer.

- We are in the middle of a language crisis.
- Our once great language is now in a state of advanced decay.
- While our teens continue to spend their lives on digital devices, our language will continue to fall apart.
- You know the story: the more Americanisms we import, the more diluted our own language becomes.

The way in which the target audience is addressed is an important aspect of how a writer can express ideas about language in the kinds of texts we are

4 Attitudes to Language

considering in this chapter. A writer who positions themselves as an expert, addressing the readers from a position of knowledge and expertise, might hope to impress a reader into accepting their argument. Meanwhile, another writer may choose to present themselves as just like 'us', grouping and aligning them with their perception of who 'we' might be. If readers accept the position of the writer (the interpersonal function), they might be more willing to accept the version of events or the representation being offered of the topic via the ideational function. Addressing people in a way that makes them feel included or special is one way to win them over to the ideas presented to them.

> **ACTIVITY 4.3**
> Text analysis
> Read Text 4E and Text 4F, which are taken from articles about language change. Think about the ways in which the writers position themselves in relation to the readers through address and pronouns.

Text 4E

> While waiting in line at the mall the other day, I ended up chatting briefly with the woman standing next to me, who turned out to be a fellow grammar enthusiast.
>
> (Yes, we exist. No, we don't get invited to many parties.)
>
> Together we lamented the fact that the absolutely unforgivable sin of homophonic confusion – in this case, the constant misuse of "your" and "you're" – seems to be rampant, and for a while we revelled in our own grammatical superiority. However, my companion then went on to blame the rise of technology – in this case, the prevalence of cellphones and online communication – for this heinous gap in the next generation's knowledge.
>
> Extract from 'English can absorb assault from texting', Shannon Corregan (*Times Colonist*, 9 March 2012)

Text 4F

> The Oxford Dictionaries Online have announced plans to include a variety of new, shall we say, colloquial words to their online collection, including slang words such as vom, selfie, unlike, digital detox, food baby and more. Sadly these are not misprints, nor has Word accidentally changed misspelt words into a seemingly-foreign language. These are in fact the pitiful emblems of the current young generation's contribution to language. My generation. I am 20.

Among the new additions, 'twerking' has taken centre stage. I actually had to Google this word yesterday when investigating why Miley Cyrus was said to have 'twerked' at the MTV video music awards.

The official definition reads: 'Twerk, v.: dance to popular music in a sexually provocative manner involving thrusting hip movements and a low, squatting stance.' Right.

Regardless, the future of the English language looks bleak.

As a member of the younger generation, partly responsible for these linguistic calamities, I can only apologise. I am embarrassed and ashamed. It doesn't exactly reflect well on young people that the new additions are mostly related to image, reputation and sex. Instead of creating words to improve our ability to communicate and express ourselves, these words simply promulgate an unhealthy culture obsessed with being seen in the right places and knowing who's doing what.

It's already a constant battle for young people to prove we're not all apathetic, ASBO-wielding yobs who can't communicate properly. These recent additions to the dictionary certainly do us no favours. Comments on Twitter and online today have enhanced our image problem. One online user wrote 'no wonder there is so much youth unemployment'; whilst another tweeted 'it's over. They've won'.

ASBO-wielding yob an aggressive youth with a court order restricting harmful behaviour

> Extract from 'Twerking, selfie and unlike? Young people don't speak like that – I should know', Isabelle Kerr (*The Telegraph*, 28 August 2013)

4.3.4 Patterns

Texts operate as coherent pieces of work, rather than just short chunks of language, so another aspect to focus on when analysing language discourses is to consider patterns and structures within texts. These could take some of the following forms:

- repetition of words, phrases, metaphors and themes
- repeated grammatical structures
- contrasting words, phrases, metaphors and themes
- recognisable parts or sections to the text
- signposting and reference between sections of a text.

Repetition can draw a reader's attention to a key theme in a text and can take many forms. On a simple level, the repetition of key words and phrases can

4 Attitudes to Language

help establish an argument, but on a more complex level, the repetition of grammatical structures – where the syntax remains the same but the words used to fill syntactical slots change – can help establish a template. Such a template can then help control what is expected to appear in each slot. Look at the following sentences and think about what you might expect to appear in the slots left empty:

- Your tea may have been picked.
- Your sugar may have been harvested.
- Your _____ may have been _____.

In each case, you would expect to insert a noun or noun phrase in the first slot and a main verb in the second. You are also 'primed' to expect similar kinds of words to those that have appeared before. It is therefore unlikely that the noun 'happiness' and the verb 'demolished' would appear in the third sentence.

Interestingly, such grammatical templates can themselves represent the world in ways that might be challenged. A slogan used on a poster by the UK Conservative Party (the Tories) in the run-up to the 1983 election (see Figure 4.1) stated (next to a picture of a young black man in a suit):

Labour says he's black.

Tories say he's British.

Figure 4.1: Poster from Conservative Party's 1983 election campaign

The slots at the beginning of the sentence set up what appear to be a pair of opposites (opposing political parties: Labour and the Conservatives) and the final slot looks to be doing the same. But are 'black' and 'British' opposing terms? Hardly. The grammatical frame sets up a false opposition between the two terms. Of course, someone can be black and British, just as they can be black and French or white and Dutch. It is also telling that the man's ethnicity is defined by someone else, rather than foregrounding his views. The grammatical structure helps to impose a way of reading that directs the reader into a particular point of view: that the two terms are mutually exclusive and you can't be one as well as the other.

When applied to language discourses, such patterns can also work to establish ways of viewing language change and variation that might not necessarily be the only ways to see the issue. For example:

- Language is not improving; it is decaying.
- Just as texting damaged young people's literacy ten years ago, social media platforms are now damaging today's teens.

While the central arguments here are certainly worth critiquing, the grammatical structures help to reinforce them. In the first example, the framing of the debate as either being about 'improving' or 'decaying' (with no other options) is partly due to the parallel structure of subject–verb in both clauses, perhaps also assisted by the repetition of the present progressive verb phrase structure (*is* verb + *-ing*). In the second example, the clause structure, where the subordinate clause (using the subordinating conjunction *as*) comes first, establishing a proposition for the second, main clause to follow, is important to the representation of language as something under threat. Of course, the first clause – it could be argued – is simply untrue and any subsequent clause that follows on from it will therefore be equally untrue.

Beyond individual words, phrases, clauses and sentences, and beyond grammatical and lexical patterning in texts, writers can also use the overall structure of a text to help establish an argument and present views about language.

Take, for example, the full text of Text 4D, which you looked at earlier in this chapter. Look at the way the writer, Shannon Corregan, uses the structure of the text to establish a prescriptive viewpoint which she then rebuts throughout the rest of the text. As you read Text 4G, try to address the following points:

- Identify the point in the article where the writer changes the perspective and reveals her true views.
- Look back to see if you can identify any hints or foreshadowing of her real views.
- Think about the kinds of evidence used to support the views offered in the text and how you might evaluate the overall argument.

4 Attitudes to Language

> **KEY TERM**
>
> **Foreshadowing:** a device in which hints are given of events to come so that the reader can predict (or often fear) what might happen in the story

Text 4G

While waiting in line at the mall the other day, I ended up chatting briefly with the woman standing next to me, who turned out to be a fellow grammar enthusiast.

(Yes, we exist. No, we don't get invited to many parties.)

Together we lamented the fact that the absolutely unforgivable sin of homophonic confusion – in this case, the constant misuse of "your" and "you're" – seems to be rampant, and for a while we revelled in our own grammatical superiority. However, my companion then went on to blame the rise of technology – in this case, the prevalence of cellphones and online communication – for this heinous gap in the next generation's knowledge.

This is an oft-cited complaint, and certainly it makes sense (on the surface, at least) to say that the rise of texting is creating a generation of young people whose standards for the basic tools of communication – spelling, grammar, sentence structure, all that good stuff – are rapidly decreasing.

As a space apparently without rules and regulations, it seems as though literacy standards would instantly dissolve on the Internet. Text messaging also seems a likely candidate for the decline of the English language, since the physical constraints of a phone's keyboard make brevity a bonus, often via unconventional spelling.

If any technological advancement is warping our children's ability to spell, the argument goes, it must be text messaging.

But I disagree.

First of all, it's important to disabuse ourselves of the idea that we're battling an ignorance epidemic, because we're not. In fact, kids are getting smarter every generation – studies have shown that IQ rates are rising, and have been steadily rising across the Western world since 1914.

And when it comes to literacy specifically, Victoria boasts an incredibly vibrant and creative writing culture in which young people are directly and actively involved. A remarkably high percentage of young people in Victoria have been engaged in literacy projects at one point in their lives, through library programs or poetry clubs or youth-focused writing journals, such as the Claremont Review.

Furthermore, at the level of anecdotal evidence, I don't think a person my age has ever worked in a fast-food environment where the teenagers at the bottom didn't have better spelling and grammar than at least some of the middle-aged managers at the top.

So this isn't a case of "kids these days." Instead, we need to make a distinction between ignorance of the rules of spelling and grammar – which is not new, and is hardly generational – and the real fallout of technological advancements in communication, which is the creative and informed misuse of language.

English is a remarkably malleable language. It robs from whomever and wherever it can in order to adapt. If languages went to kindergarten, English would be the one stealing the other languages' milk money and pushing them around on the playground. English is continually evolving and changing, and nowhere is that more apparent than through the prevalence of Internet-born "memespeak" and text messaging.

"Thru" has replaced "through," just as "plow" replaced "plough" decades before. This is not the end of the world. Emoticons are making their way into professional and business emails, but they're actually helpful tools: Although they had their start as goofy wingdings, they help to clarify the tone of otherwise indecipherable walls of text. Emoticons are such a staple of online communication that my cellphone, which lacks a bracket symbol, is actually a hindrance to my communication. "I'll be there" is curt, even rude, without a little :) to reassure your reader.

I know there are some people who will forever cringe when they hear a person say "lol" out loud, and for whom text abbreviations will forever be a sign of poor intelligence, but I argue the opposite.

While, for reasons of sheer obnoxiousness, I would be interested in banning anyone under the age of 16 from using a cellphone, illiteracy has nothing to do with the prevalence of texting.

Our technological advancements have given us new ways to communicate. Our language is changing on us, and that isn't a bad thing. It always has, and it always will.

'English can absorb assault from texting', Shannon Corregan
(*Times Colonist*, 9 March, 2012)

In this chapter you have looked at a selection of different methods for analysing language discourses and articles about language. The last main task for you to do now is to study a full text and apply what you have learned.

4 Attitudes to Language

> **ACTIVITY 4.4**
> **Evaluating views**
>
> Read Text 4H, which is the complete article by Lindsay Johns, a journalist who works with young people in Peckham, an area in south-east London. Summarise the key arguments he makes and identify the main points about the following:
>
> - how some young people use language and some of the features of this 'ghetto grammar'
> - the advantages and disadvantages of certain forms of language
> - his solution for improving young people's language and prospects.
>
> Use the toolkit suggested in this chapter to analyse and evaluate the views Johns puts forward and the language he uses to do it. How convincing are the arguments in this text?

Text 4H

In the wake of the riots, last Thursday evening, there was only one topic of conversation among the young people I mentor in Peckham. Thankfully, none of my mentees were involved in the disturbances. Yet almost all told me they had received the mass BBM broadcasts, written in street slang, inviting them to join in the thuggery.

The English language is an incredibly rich inheritance. Yet it is being squandered by so many young people of all races and backgrounds. Across London and other cities it is increasingly fashionable for them to speak in an inarticulate slang full of vacuous words such as "innit" and wilful distortions like "arks" for "ask" or tedious double negatives.

It's not a question of being a staunch lexical purist. It's about our attitude to young people and how we educate them. Language is power. The ability for young people to communicate articulately and intelligently is of huge importance, not only for themselves but also for the way in which they are perceived by others.

Their educational opportunities and job prospects are all directly affected by the way they choose to speak. Moreover, the more we are unable to express our feelings through words, the more frustrated we get.
For young men and women in the inner-city, that can only be a dangerous thing.

Language discourses

So in my mentoring work I have zero tolerance towards inchoate street slang. As I constantly tell these young people, words are the best weapon you can have in your mental arsenal. Each week in Peckham we have a vocabulary slot, where we teach five new words. Be it ubiquitous, judicious, sardonic, ephemeral or plethora, we teach these young people words which can assist them, be it in GCSE English essays or everyday conversation.

Young people speaking street patois is a spectacular own goal. True, the patois limits their conversation to a select coterie of other young people, making it hard to penetrate if you don't know the lingo. But in so doing, young people are effectively rendering themselves unintelligible to – and often unemployable by – mainstream adult society. This is really why street slang is anathema to me: it is reckless self-sabotage.

Some educators take a position of cultural relativism. They assert the legitimacy and value of street talk, or at the very least, the importance of teaching young people to "code switch" – how to differentiate in which milieu it is socially acceptable.

I have no time for such an approach. In my experience, young people find it very hard to code switch. Text-speak, poor grammar and street patois routinely pervade the essays I set them, let alone their conversations with me.

Acceptance of "ghetto grammar" amounts to a betrayal of young people, trapping them in stereotypes. The young people I mentor are not stupid – yet their street slang makes them sound stupid and uneducated.

The better they speak, the more others – especially in positions of authority – will be inclined to take them seriously. Embracing street slang leads to disenfranchisement, marginalisation and ultimately the dole queue. Embracing "proper English" unlocks an intellectual feast.

But to help them do so, we must confront this insulting and demeaning acceptance of street slang. We owe it to them: as adults, we do have a duty of linguistic care.

'Ghetto grammar robs the young of a proper voice', Lindsay Johns (*Evening Standard*, 16 August 2011)

4 Attitudes to Language

> **RESEARCH QUESTION**
> **Critical evaluation**
>
> Linguists and language teachers have responded to several of Lindsay Johns' arguments and you can find out more in the following links. Read some of these responses and then evaluate which views you think are most convincing.
>
> - This link is a response from the linguist Paul Kerswill to a BBC lecture by Lindsay Johns on the same topic: www.cambridge.org/links/escatt6010
> - This link is a piece by linguist Rob Drummond in response to the same Radio 4 lecture: www.cambridge.org/links/escatt6004

4.4 Further exploration and investigation

Throughout this book you have looked at different views about the English language. Many of these views, as you have seen, have been around for centuries and recur in slightly different contexts. Arguments about technology's influence on language have raged since writing started to take over from speech as the standard form of the language and as the keyboard took over from the pen as the main means of 'writing'. The views often fit into very familiar patterns of concern, even using many of the same discourses of decline, decay and invasion.

Each of the chapters in this book has hopefully provided you with ideas for pursuing further study of the subject, but one important area is the 'Language investigation' and this is something to look at briefly here in the context of attitudes to change and variation.

The 'Language investigation' is a piece of student-led research that involves you choosing a topic area, setting a research question, collecting data and analysing it to help you answer your question. It is very likely that you will be asked, at some point in your studies, to undertake some of your own research on an aspect of the English language.

When looking at attitudes to change and variation, some of the following suggestions might offer you the scope to carry out investigations of your own.

Language discourses

This is not an exhaustive list but gives you a few starting points. You could investigate:

- how national and local newspapers and media outlets represent a local variety of language
- how changes in modes of communication (telephone, telegram, text message, social media) are reported on at the time
- how varieties of non-Standard English are judged by different age groups
- how complaints about language change are phrased over the years in letters to the editors in national newspapers
- how regional accents and dialects are judged
- how new entries to dictionaries are discussed in online forums or as online comments to news articles.

Wider reading

You can find out more about the topics in this chapter by reading the following:

Aitchison, J. (2012) *Language Change: Progress or Decay?* (Fourth edition). Cambridge: Cambridge University Press.

Baker, P. (2008) *Sexed Texts: Language, Gender and Sexuality*. London: Equinox.

Fairclough, N. (2014) *Language and Power* (Third edition). London: Routledge.

Goddard, A. and Carey, N. (2017) *Discourse: the basics*. London: Routledge.

Greene, R.L. (2011) *You Are What You Speak: Grammar Grouches, Language Laws and the Politics of Identity*. New York: Delacorte Press.

Hitchings, H. (2011) *The Language Wars: A History of Proper English*. London: John Murray.

In a blog post on *Separated by a Common Language*, Lynne Murphy describes a quick piece of research that she carried out into who or what is seen to be to blame for the supposed destruction/decline/ruination of English. You can read more about it here: https://separatedbyacommonlanguage.blogspot.co.uk/2014/05/who-is-ruiningspoilingdestroying-english.html

Ideas and answers

Chapter 1

Activity 1.2

Johns puts forward very different ideas about what Standard and non-Standard English can offer its speakers:

- Standard English: opportunities in employment and education; being taken seriously by those in authority; intellectual advancement

- Non-Standard English: being treated as stereotypes; the appearance of ignorance and stupidity; being outside the mainstream of society and deprived of its economic, educational and social benefits. He sees those who 'allow' this to happen as betraying young people.

Activity 1.3

Benefits of a standard:

- An agreed set of 'rules' or conventions that all can follow

- A shared language, allowing intelligibility for all

- A model for learners to aim towards

- A 'level playing field' that all learners can have access to, whatever their language backgrounds

- A link to the history and traditions of a language

Drawbacks of a standard:

- If one form of a language is viewed as a standard, all other forms are viewed as potentially sub-standard

- The issue of who decides what becomes the standard form

- The standard form could exclude those who do not use it in their day-to-day lives.

- Standards are often used to judge and discriminate, rather than unite

Activity 1.4

Spelling has always been a problematic area for English because of its mixture of rules based on sounds of words, historical origins of those words and the largely spoken nature of much early English. Out of all the different aspects of English

Ideas and answers

use among individuals, spelling is often one of the most varied, particularly when aspects such as English being used as a second language, or technology and different audiences are considered.

Activity 1.5

Some of the most frequent recent patterns in word formation have been blends and compounds. However, in previous decades, initialisms and acronyms have featured a little more heavily. The lists of words that you find will no doubt contain some interesting and bizarre (and occasionally useful) new terms, but they will usually follow fairly familiar patterns of word formation.

Activity 1.6

Some ideas about each of the examples are suggested here.

- **terrible:** once meant causing terror, but has semantically weakened to mean something closer to just 'bad'.
- **heavy:** still has a primary meaning connected to weight but this has broadened to mean serious, profound or dark (e.g. 'The conversation turned to heavier topics').
- **cute:** once used to mean sharp, perceptive and intelligent (from a shortened version of 'acute') but has semantically shifted to mean attractive or 'nice'.
- **silly:** once meant happy, lucky and even blessed, but has acquired unfavourable connotations to mean lacking intelligence and insight. Probably linked to a rather cynical view that happy people are a little naïve and therefore not very intelligent!

Activity 1.7

Much of the coverage of vocal fry has been negative, likening it to a speech disorder, an illness or a silly and faddish affectation. One argument that often appears is that it is (another) feature of language that young women should avoid if they wish to be taken seriously. However, men who use vocal fry are rarely remarked upon and it is probably as common in men as women.

Chapter 3

Activity 3.1

Some ideas for each example are provided here.

- *We was just sat there, waiting.* The use of 'was' here would be seen as an example of non-standard concordance (or subject-verb agreement) where the standard 'were' would normally appear. In some varieties of English, 'sat' is used as a participle form of the verb *to* 'sit', rather than the more standard 'sitting' usage.

Attitudes to Language

- *Your girl's got bare skills on Fifa, innit?* In terms of grammar, tag questions such as 'isn't it?' and 'don't you?', normally vary according to the subject of the verb. In this example 'innit?' is being used to refer to a person, where you might normally see 'isn't she?' appearing. In terms of semantics, 'bare' has a different meaning here to the standard 'minimal' or 'naked' and instead means 'a lot' or 'many'.

- *How much did you get? I got nowt.* 'Nowt' is a common northern English dialect term for nothing ('owt' being its opposite, 'something').

- *She run fast fast.* In some forms of world Englishes and pidgins, two adverbs (or adjectives) are used together to mean 'very' (e.g. 'fast fast' for 'very fast' or 'big big' to mean 'very big'). As with the first example, the grammar of 'she run' is non-standard and you would normally see 'she run<u>s</u>' or 'she <u>ran</u>' here, depending on the tense.

- *I ain't seen nobody come down here today. They come down yesterday but not today.* There are several features of non-standard grammar here. Multiple negation is used in 'I ain't seen nobody', where Standard English would only mark the negative once ('I saw nobody' or 'I didn't see anybody'), 'come' is being used as a non-standard past tense where 'came' would be more usual, while 'ain't' is a very widely-used contraction, taking the place of 'I am not' but is here used to mean 'I haven't'.

- *Do you want butter on your cob, me duck?* Terms of endearment and address vary around the world and 'me duck' is a familiar term in the English East Midlands. Other terms such as 'me lover', 'my dear', 'dude', 'mate' and just 'yo' might be found elsewhere. Words for different types of food vary around the English-speaking world too, so bread rolls have a variety of different names in the UK ('cob', 'bap', 'stotty', 'barmcake' being just a few).

- *Nobody else thought he were funny, but I thought he were a right laff.* A different form of non-standard subject-verb agreement can be seen with 'he were', where 'he was' would be more standard and 'laff' suggests a particular accent (in the UK, a northern rather than southern pronunciation of the /a/ sound. More details of UK phonological diversity can be found in the Cambridge Topics in English Language series, *Language Diversity and World Englishes*.

- *This boy was like 'Where are you from?' and I was like 'Bow' and this is him 'Bow? These ain't your endz then' and this is me 'I'm visiting my cousin innit'.* This example of what might be termed Multicultural London English (MLE) uses several different features, where quotatives such as 'was like' and 'this is him/me' introduce speech or actions. 'Endz' is a slang term used to mean area or neighbourhood. 'Innit' is being used as an invariant tag question, as you saw in the second example above.

Activity 3.2

If you have listened to the clips of RP, you will have a good idea of what it sounds like. It is also useful to read the other material on the British Library website that describes the sounds of RP and to visit John Wells' Phonetic Blog (www.cambridge.org/links/escatt6011).

Ideas and answers

Activity 3.3
- Opinions vary about accents, but many accents in the UK are not liked even by those who have them.
- Birmingham (Brummie) and Bristol fare badly.
- Newcastle (Geordie) and Manchester (Mancunian) fare better.
- Accents used in advertising can have an impact on how the message of the advert is responded to.

Activity 3.4
Pros:
- Development of clarity and power, according to the company
- Helps develop confidence and advances career opportunities
- A process that can be taught

Cons:
- Loss of original identity
- Adoption of a bland, homogeneous variety
- Pressure to conform to others' prejudices

Activity 3.5
- The school claims to be 'improving language skills'.
- It says regional phrases are 'damaging' to pupils.
- The school wants children to be able to switch between local and standard forms.
- Some parents object and see it as restrictive as well as dismissive of local identity and culture.
- The school's view might be seen as patronising and counter-productive.
- An issue is being made out of something that most children do not have a problem with.

Activity 3.6
By reading Murphy's and Liberman's responses to Engel's text, you will get a clear idea of the objections these two experts raise to the examples and arguments made in the original text.

Chapter 4

Activity 4.3

Corregan's article uses an anecdotal style in the first person to establish a voice. She positions herself as self-deprecating and aware of how 'nerdy' an interest in grammar might appear. She seems to align herself with the woman in the mall, but signals her distance from some of the later opinions with devices such as the verb 'seems', the adverb 'However' and the hyperbole of 'heinous' – all suggesting that she doesn't share the woman's prescriptive views despite their initial bonding over grammar.

Kerr's article uses the first person and, by signalling her membership of the group she is criticising, she suggests a distancing of herself from her peers. She again suggests that she is not the same as others by claiming she had to Google the meaning of a slang term, and in her apology on their behalf for the slang use she says young people are responsible for.

Activity 4.4

See the feedback for Activity 1.2 in Chapter 1 for some initial observations. More detailed discussion of Johns' position and arguments can be found in two blog posts:

- www.cambridge.org/links/escatt6004
- www.cambridge.org/links/escatt6010

References

Aitchison, J. (1997) *The Language Web: The Power and Problem of Words. The 1996 BBC Reith Lectures*. Cambridge: Cambridge University Press.

Aitchison, J. (2012) 'Reith Lectures: Is our language in decay'. *Independent*, 7 February 1996. Available at: www.independent.co.uk/life-style/reith-lectures-is-our-language-in-decay-1317695.html

Baron, N. (2008) *Always On: Language in an Online and Mobile World*. Oxford: Oxford University Press.

Baron, D. (2009) *A Better Pencil: Readers, Writers and the Digital Revolution*. Oxford: Oxford University Press.

Baugh and Cable (2012) *A History of the English Language* (Sixth edition). London: Routledge.

Burridge, K. (2004) *Weeds in the Garden of Words*. Cambridge: Cambridge University Press.

Cameron, D. (2015a) 'Just don't do it'. Language: a feminist guide, 5 July. Available at: https://debuk.wordpress.com/2015/07/05/just-dont-do-it/

Cameron, D. (2015b) 'A response to Naomi Wolf' Language: a feminist guide, 26 July. Available at: https://debuk.wordpress.com/2015/07/26/a-response-to-naomi-wolf/

Chatfield, T. (2013) *Netymology*. London: Quercus.

Clark, U. (2017) 'You are what you speak'. 31 March. Available at: www.aston.ac.uk/research/case-studies/you-are-what-you-speak/

Clayton, D. and Drummond, R. (2018) *Language Diversity*. Cambridge: Cambridge University Press.

Crystal, D. (1997) *The Cambridge Encyclopedia of the English Language*. Cambridge: Cambridge University Press.

Crystal, D. (2005) *The Stories of English*. London: Penguin.

Crystal, D. (2008) '2b or not 2b?', *The Guardian*, 5 July . Available at: www.theguardian.com/books/2008/jul/05/saturdayreviewsfeatres.guardianreview

Deutscher, G. (2006) *The Unfolding of Language*. London: Arrow Books.

Drummond, R. (2016) 'Slang shouldn't be banned … it should be celebrated, innit'. *The Conversation*, 3 May. Available at: http://theconversation.com/slang-shouldnt-be-banned-it-should-be-celebrated-innit-58672

Edwards, K. (2014) 'Shut yer face! I'm fed up being ridiculed for my regional accent in academia', *The Telegraph*, 9 December. Available at: www.telegraph.co.uk/women/womens-life/11270980/Britishuniversities-Im-fed-up-of-being-ridiculed-for-my-regional-accent.html

Engel, M. (2010) 'Say no to the get-go! Americanisms swamping English, so wake up and smell the coffee'. Daily Mail Online, 29 May. Available at: www.dailymail.co.uk/news/article-1282449/Americanisms-swamping-English-wake-smell-coffee.html

Engel, M. (2011) 'Viewpoint: Why do some Americanisms irritate people?' BBC News, 13 July. Available at:www.bbc.co.uk/news/14130942

Fairclough, N. (1989) *Language and Power*. London: Routledge.

Fairclough, N. (2014) *Language and Power* (Third edition). London: Routledge.

Goddard, A. and Carey, N. (2017) *Discourse: the basics*. London: Routledge.

Graddol, D., Leith, D., Swann, J. (eds) (2006) *Changing English*. London: Routledge.

Greene, R.L. (2011) *You Are What You Speak: Grammar Grouches, Language Laws and the Politics of Identity*. New York: Delacorte Press.

Hardaker, C. (2013) 'Uh ... not to be nitpicky ... but ... the past tense of drag is dragged, not drug: an overview of trolling strategies', *Journal of Language Aggression and Conflict*. 1 (1): 57–86.

Herring, S. (1996) *Computer-mediated Communication: Linguistic, Social, and Cross-cultural Perspectives*. London: John Benjamins Publishing Company.

Hilmarsdóttir, G. (2006) 'Estuary English – The New Classless Accent?' (dissertation). Available at: www.phon.ucl.ac.uk/home/estuary/

Hitchings, H. (2011a) *The Language Wars: A History of Proper English*. London: John Murray.

Hitchings, H. (2011b) 'At war with the pedants', emagazine 53: 26–27.

Holmes, J. (2008) *An Introduction to Sociolinguistics*. Harlow: Pearson Education.

Honey, J. (1989) *Does Accent Matter?: The Pygmalion Factor*. London: Faber and Faber.

Howse, C. (2010) 'Google the term of the decade? It's a war of words out there'. *The Telegraph*, 14 January. Available at: www.telegraph.co.uk/comment/columnists/christopherhowse/6990563/Google-the-term-of-the-decade-Its-a-war-of-words-out-there.html

Hudson, R. (2004) *Sociolinguistics*. Cambridge: Cambridge University Press.

Humphrys, J. (2007) 'I h8 txt msgs: How texting is wrecking our language'. *Daily Mail*, 24 September. Available at: www.dailymail.co.uk/news/article-483511/I-h8-txt-msgs-How-texting-wrecking-language.html

ITV/ComRes (2013) 'ITV Tonight Regional Accents Survey'. 24 September. Available at: www.comresglobal.com/polls/itv-tonight-regional-accents-survey/

Kaplan, A. (2016) *Women Talk More Than Men... And Other Myths About Language Explained*. Cambridge: Cambridge University Press.

Krupnick, M. (2010) 'Texting slang invading academic work'. *The Seattle Times,* 14 April. Available at: www.seattletimes.com/life/lifestyle/texting-slang-invading-academic-work/

References

Liberman, M. (2011) 'Peeve of the week: 20% correct'. 16 July. Available at: http://languagelog.ldc.upenn.edu/nll/?p=3271

Lusher, A. (2015) 'Emojis now more popular than acronyms, says Instagram'. *Independent*, 4 May. Available at: www.independent.co.uk/life-style/gadgets-and-tech/news/omg-internet-slang-acronyms-being-replaced-by-cartoon-style-emoji-pictograms-say-instagram-10224416.html

Luu, C. (2017) 'Very British villains (and other Anglo-Saxon attitudes to accents)', *Daily JStor*, 18 January. Available at: https://daily.jstor.org/very-british-villains-and-other-anglo-saxon-attitudes-to-accents/

Marsh, D. (2013) *For Who the Bell Tolls*. London: Guardian Faber Publishing.

Marsh, S. (2006) 'The rise of the interrogatory statement'. *The Times*, 28 March. Available at: www.thetimes.co.uk/tto/law/columnists/article2045829.ece (Note: you need to register to access the full article.)

McCulloch, G. (2016) 'A Linguist Explains Emoji and What Language Death Actually Looks Like'. *The Toast*, 29 June. Available at: http://the-toast.net/2016/06/29/a-linguist-explains-emoji-and-what-language-death-actually-looks-like/

McWhorter, J. (2016) *Words on the Move*. New York: Henry Holt and Company.

Metcalf, A. (2016) 'Hey, You Guys! Listen Up!' *The Chronicle of Higher Education*, 27 November. Available at: www.chronicle.com/blogs/linguafranca/2016/11/27/hey-you-guys-listen-up/

Milroy, J. and Milroy, L. (1985) *Authority in Language: Investigating Standard English*. Cambridge: Cambridge University Press.

Nevalainen, T. and Tieken-Boon Van Ostade, I. (2006) 'Standardisation'. In R. Hogg and D. Denison (eds) *A History of the English Language* Cambridge: Cambridge University Press, p. 275.

Nicoll, J. D. (1990) 'The King's English'. Newsgroup: rec.arts.sf-lovers

Plester, B., Wood, C. and Joshi, P. (2009) 'Exploring the relationship between children's knowledge of text message abbreviations and school literacy outcomes', *British Journal of Developmental Psychology* 27 (1): 145–161.

Rollins, S. (2013) 'How the wrong definition of 'literally' sneaked into the dictionary'. *The Week,* 6 March. Available at: http://theweek.com/articles/466957/how-wrong-definition-literally-sneaked-into-dictionary

Rudder, C. (2014) 'Is Twitter bad for language? Statistical analysis says no'. HuffPost, 10 September. Available at: www.huffingtonpost.com/2014/09/10/twitter-language-book_n_5786556.html

Rundell, M. (2011) 'This will literally have you in stitches'. Macmillan Dictionary Blog. Available at: www.macmillandictionaryblog.com/this-will-literally-have-you-in-stitches

Saraceni, M. (2008) 'English as a lingua franca: between form and function', *English Today*, 24: 2.

Schegloff, E. (1986) 'The routine as achievement', *Human Studies*, 9: 111–151.

Schnoebelen, T. (2016) 'Emojis are becoming a bigger part of conversation ;)'. Words you'll hear, 28 February. Available at: www.npr.org/2016/02/28/468483894/emojis-are-becoming-a-bigger-part-of-conversation

Snell, J. (2013) 'Saying no to "gizit" is plain prejudice'. *Independent*, 10 February. Available at: www.independent.co.uk/voices/comment/saying-no-to-gizit-is-plain-prejudice-8488358.html

Stewart, M. A., Ryan, E. B. and Giles, H. (1985), 'Accent and social class effects on status and solidarity evaluations', *Personality and Social Psychology Bulletin*, 11: 98–105.

Sutherland, J. (2002) 'Cn u txt?' *The Guardian,* 11 November. Available at: www.theguardian.com/technology/2002/nov/11/mobilephones2

Tagg, C. (2015) *Exploring Digital Communication*. London: Routledge.

Thorne, S. (2003) 'Brummie sings to foreign ears'. *Times Higher Education*, 5 September. Available at: www.timeshighereducation.com/news/brummie-sings-to-foreign-ears/178993.article (Note: you need to register to access the full article.)

Wolf, N. (2015) 'Young women, give up the vocal fry and reclaim your strong female voice'. *The Guardian*, 24 July. Available at: https://www.theguardian.com/commentisfree/2015/jul/24/vocal-fry-strong-female-voice

YouGov (2014)'"Brummie" is the least attractive accent'. Available at: https://yougov.co.uk/news/2014/12/09/accent-map2/

Glossary

accommodation theory: how people adjust their speech behaviours to match others. This can be aspects of accent, grammar, vocabulary and even the style of speech delivery

amelioration: the process of a word's meaning changing and picking up more positive connotations over time

aspect: how language indicates whether an action or event is or has been completed or ongoing; in English, this is usually separated into perfective or progressive

blending: the process of word creation by combining two elements of other words (e.g. 'bromance' = *bro*ther + *romance*; 'brunch' = *br*eakfast + l*unch*)

borrowing: the process of taking a word from another language and inserting into the lexicon of another

broadening: the process of a word's meanings becoming more generalised over time

code-switching: speakers who speak two dialects of a language or two entirely different languages, switching from one to the other depending on whom they are talking to or what they wish to accomplish

compounding: the process of word creation by combining two existing words either as a new single word, hyphenated word or noun phrase (e.g. 'laptop' = *lap* + *top*; 'user-friendly' = *user* + *friendly*)

computer-mediated communication (CMC): any form of communication that uses the medium of a keyboard or digital device, rather than being spoken or written

contronym: a word that can mean one thing and its exact opposite at the same time

convergence: how speakers move speech styles and patterns to more closely match those of other speakers

conversion: the process of changing the grammatical function of a word (e.g. turning a noun into a verb or vice versa)

Critical Discourse Analysis: an approach to the study of both written and spoken language focusing on the ways that power is enacted

declinism: a tendency noted by Robert Lane Greene for prescriptivists to view language as being in state of constant decline from a once great peak

descriptivism: a way of viewing language as being standard or non-standard, not making judgements about correctness

dialect levelling: the process by which language forms of different parts of the country converge and become more similar over time, with the loss of regional features and reduced diversity of language

Attitudes to Language

dialect: language associated with a particular locality, region or geographical area

divergence: when an individual changes their language choices (usually temporarily) to become more dissimilar to another individual or group

emoji: a term to describe visual icons (representations of facial expressions, actions and objects) used in social media messaging

filler: a word or sound used to fill a gap in spoken language (e.g. *um, err, uh, like*)

flipping: a term used to describe a rapid semantic change in a word from one meaning to its opposite or near opposite

foreshadowing: a device in which hints are given of events to come so that the reader can predict (or often fear) what might happen in the story

grammatical variation: how varieties of English use different grammatical structures to create meaning

high-rising terminals (HRT)/uptalk: a way of speaking in which the intonation pattern moves up towards the end of a declarative utterance

idiolect: variation in language use associated with an individual's personalised 'speech style'

intelligibility: the ability to be understood and comprehended

lexicon: the vocabulary of a language

loan word: a word that has been borrowed

modal auxiliary verb: a modal auxiliary is a verb that works alongside other verbs to express degrees of certainty, obligation, possibility and permission

narrowing: the process of a word's meanings becoming more specialised over time

neologism: a completely new word

orthographical variation: how the use of symbols, letters and spellings varies among language users

patois: the dialect of a particular group, especially one with low status in relation to the standard language

pejoration: the process of a word's meaning changing and picking up more negative connotations over time

phatic interaction: the type of exchange which is redundant in terms of meaning but socially significant; it includes 'friendly noises' like 'Morning', 'Nice day' and 'How's things?'

phonological variation: how the sounds of English vary among different speakers of English

pragmatics: the study of language as it is used in a social context

prescriptivism: a way of viewing language as correct or incorrect, prescribing a 'correct' way to use language

quotative: a language device used to convey what was said, thought or done in an interaction (e.g. she *said*... or she *was like*...)

rising intonation: using a rising tone as an utterance ends. Generally used when asking a question, but now more prevalent in statements. Can also be referred to as high-rising terminals or uptalk

Glossary

semantic variation: how word meanings vary from place to place and group to group

sociolect: language associated with a particular social group

style shifting: moving between different levels of formality or register in the same language

synthetic personalisation: a technique identified by the linguist Norman Fairclough in which an audience is addressed in a way that suggests they are known as individuals

tense: how language indicates when an event or action took place. In English, this is usually defined as past or present (and there is some debate over whether English has a genuine future tense)

vocal fry: a way of speaking that constricts the vocal cords and creates a creaking, low frequency sound

Index

Page numbers in italics are figures; with 't' are tables.

abbreviations in texting 35–6
accents *see* regional variations
address 84–5
American English 68–71

Birmingham accent 4, 50, 53, 54, 55t, *56*, 57t, 60, 62

changing English 14–24, *20*
  see also technology
class (social) 53–4, 58–60
code-switching 66–7
complaints about English 12–13
computer-mediated communication (CMC) 14, 41–2
  see also texting technologies
Critical Discourse Analysis (CDA) 74

declinist views of English 15–16, 78
dialects 6, 10, 13
discourse 74–5
  describing language 75–9
  language toolkits 79–92

education, and non-Standard English 64–7
emoji/emojis 17, 42–5, *43–4*
emoticons 39, 43, 89
Estuary English 58–60, *59*
ethnicity 60

foreshadowing 87–9

ghetto grammar 7–8, 75–6, 90–1
grammar, and discourse 80
grammatical variation 3, 34, 48

high-rising terminals (HRT) 21–4

ideational function of language 79
interpersonal function of language 79

metaphor 75
modality 82–3

modification 80–1
non-Standard English 2–3, 7–8
noun phrases 80–1

orthographical variation 4–5

patterns in texts 85–92, *86*
phonology 4, 21–4, 48
pragmatics 42, 48, 79
pronouns 83–5

Received Pronunciation (RP) 53–4, 55t, *56*, 57t, 58, 61–2
regional variations 51–67, 55t, *56*, 57t, 59
repetition in texts 85–7, *86*

semantic variation 3–4, 31–4, *32*, 48
social media 14, 34, 41–2, 43–4
  Twitter 32, *32*, 41–2
speaking technologies 28–9
spelling 9–10, 14, *15*
spoken language 13
Standard English 5–6, 8–12, *9*, 13, 51–2, 64
stereotyping, and accents 60–4
style shifting 66–7

technology 26–45, *32*
  and language change 26–31, *26*
  and new words 31–4
  and texting 34–40, *37*
texting 30–1, *32*, 34–40, *37*, 77–8
textual function of language 79
tone 42–3
Twitter 32, *32*, 41–2

uptalk 21–4

variation in language 48–50, *50*
  beyond England 67–71
  regional 51–67
verb phrases 81–2
vocabulary, change in 16–21, 31–4

words, new 31–4, *32*
writing technologies 27–8

Acknowledgements

The authors and publishers acknowledge the following sources of copyright material and are grateful for the permissions granted. While every effort has been made, it has not always been possible to identify the sources of all the material used, or to trace all copyright holders. If any omissions are brought to our notice, we will be happy to include the appropriate acknowledgements on reprinting.

Text 1A, 4A, 4I from 'Ghetto grammar robs the young of a proper voice' by Lindsay Johns, London Evening Standard, August 2011, by permission of ESI Media; Text 2A 'Texting is making English a foreign language' by Michael Deacon, The Telegraph, 2009 © Telegraph Media Group Limited 2009; Text 2B 'Is Texting Killing the English Language?' by John McWhorter on ideas. time.com Time Inc. with kind permission from John McWhorter, teacher of Linguistics at Columbia University, 2013; Text 2C from 'No, emojis aren't making our generation stupid' Paden Vaughan interview with Vyvyan Evans, Huck Magazine, 2017 © TCO London; Text 3A from 'Not all regions like to hear their own accents in ads, survey finds' by Mark Sweney and James Robinson, The Guardian 2009, Copyright Guardian News & Media Ltd 2017; Text 3B Accent Reduction and Pronunciation advert © Communicate School of English; Text 3C from ' Yow cor spaek lyuke that! West Midlands school bans pupils from using 'damaging' regional slang' by Martin Fricker © Mirror 2013; Text 3D from 'Say no to the get-go! Americanisms swamping English, so wake up and smell the coffee' by Matthew Engel in the Daily Mail online, used by permission of the author; Text 4B from 'I h8 txt msgs: How texting is wrecking our language' by John Humphrys, Daily Mail 2007 © Daily Mail via Solo Syndication; Text 4C from 'Language can't stay still - just listen to London' by Henry Hitchings, London Evening Standard, 2011, by permission of Independent Media Publishing; Text 4D, 4F, 4H from 'English Can Absorb Assault from Texting' by Shannon Corregan, Times Colonist © Times Colonist 2012; Text 4G from 'Twerking, selfie and unlike? Young people don't speak like that – I should know' by Isabelle Kerr, Telegraph, 2013© Telegraph Media Group Limited 2013

Development of this publication has made use of the Cambridge English Corpus (CEC). The CEC is a multi-billion word computer database of contemporary spoken and written English. It includes British English, American English and other varieties of English. It also includes the Cambridge Learner Corpus, developed in collaboration with Cambridge English Language Assessment. Cambridge University Press has built up the CEC to provide evidence about language use that helps to produce better language teaching materials.

Attitudes to Language

Thanks to the following for permission to reproduce images:

Cover image: Ray Wise/Getty Images; chapter opener images 1–4 Pgiam/Getty Images, Image Source/Getty Images, Timothy Kirman / EyeEm/Getty Images, blackred/Getty Images; Fig. 1.3 by xkcd.com; Fig. 2.1 GK Hart/Vikki Hart/Getty Images; Fig. 2.3a User2547783c_812/Getty Images; Fig. 2.3b ET-ARTWORKS/Getty Images; Fig. 2.4 CBS via Getty Images; Fig. 2.5 yayayoyo/Getty Images; Fig. 3.2 map recreated with permission from YouGov https://yougov.co.uk/news/2014/12/09/accent-map2; Fig. 4.1 Image Courtesy of The Advertising Archives

The publisher would like to thank the following members of The Cambridge Panel: English who assisted in reviewing this book: Anisa Ravat, Carolin Haubold and Angela Janovsky.

The author would like to thank Marcello Giovanelli for his vision for the series and his help and support with this book, my former English department colleagues at Colchester Sixth Form College for their good humour and expertise, all my (good) A level students past & present and Jo, Liam, Stan and Ruby.